Whistler and Montesquiou

The Butterfly and the Bat

Whistler, *Arrangement in Black and Gold:*
Comte Robert de Montesquiou-Fezensac,
oil, 1891–92, New York, Frick Collection

Whistler and Montesquiou

The Butterfly and the Bat

Edgar Munhall

The Frick Collection / **Flammarion**
New York and Paris

Front cover illustration: Whistler, *Arrangement in Black and Gold: Comte Robert de Montesquiou-Fezensac* (detail), oil, 1891–92, New York, Frick Collection

Back cover illustrations: (left) Sem, *Robert de Montesquiou,* color lithograph, n.d., New York, Frick Collection; (right) SPY (Leslie Ward), *A Symphony (Portrait of Whistler),* color lithograph, 1878, New York Public Library

Endpapers: C. Meunier, *Cover* for Montesquiou's *Les Chauves-Souris,* embossed leather, 1906, Paris, private collection, provenance Montesquiou

Title page illustrations: (left) Whistler, *Symphony in Grey and Green: The Ocean* (detail of butterfly signature on frame), oil, after 1866, New York, Frick Collection; (right) Leuchars & Son, London—Paris, *Silvered Embossed Bat Seal on Montesquiou's Letter Paper,* 1897, Paris, private collection

Printed and bound in France

Paperback edition: ISBN: 2-08013-578-3
Numéro d'édition: 0916
Dépôt legal February 1995

Hardcover edition: ISBN: 2-08013-577-5
Numéro d'édition: 0915
Dépôt legal February 1995

Photographic Credits

Agence Photographique de la Réunion des Musées Nationaux, Paris: 10, 21, 95, 104, 105, 106
Art Institute of Chicago: 55 (Clarence Buckingham Collection), 57 (Bryan Lathrop Collection), 59 (Arthur Jerome Eddy Memorial Collection), 96 (gift of Walter S. Brewster)
Art Museum, Princeton University: 107 (gift of J. Lionberger Davis)
Atelier 80, Paris: p. 13, 41
Bibliothèque Nationale de France, Service Photographique: 45, 71, 73, 113
Brooklyn Museum, New York: 15 (gift of A. Augustus Healy), 110, 111 (purchased by public subscription)
Carnegie Museum of Art, Pittsburgh: 124
Chrysler Museum, Norfolk, Virginia: 97
Flammarion, Paris (Frédéric Morellec): 23, 24, 29, 30, 31, 35, 39, 42, 44, 48, 50, 53, 60, 66, 67, 90, 92, 93, 94, 101, 114, 117, 118, 132
Freer Gallery of Art, Smithsonian Institution, Washington: 4, 11, 122
Frick Collection, New York (Richard di Liberto): frontispiece, 5, 12, 13, 22, 28, 37, 49, 58, 76, 77, 78, 79, 80, 81, 82, 84, 85, 86, 88, 89, 103, 112, 119, 120, 123, 125
Glasgow Art Gallery and Museum: 69

Glasgow University Library, Special Collections: 33, 36, 61, 64
Greg Heins: 74
The Hispanic Society of America, New York: 127
Houghton Library, Harvard University, Cambridge, Massachusetts: 20
Hunterian Art Gallery, University of Glasgow, Birnie Philip Bequest: 8, 9, 14, 56, 63, 91, 126
Library of Congress, Washington: 25, 26, 43, 46, 72, 83
Metropolitan Museum of Art, New York: 1 (bequest of William H. Walker, 1918, copyright 1993), 6 (The Elisha Whitelsey Collection, The Elisha Whitelsey Fund, 1957), 38 (gift of George Davis, 1948), 99 (Rogers Fund, 1937, copyright 1994), 108 (Arthur Hoppock Hearn Fund, 1916, copyright 1992), 115 (Wolfe Fund, 1913; Catharine Lorillard Wolfe Collection, copyright 1984), 129 (Rogers Fund, 1917, copyright 1990/94)
Musée de Chartres (François Velard): 40
Musée Clemenceau, Paris: 32
Museo del Prado, Madrid: 128
Museum of Art, Rhode Island School of Design: 133
Nevill Keating Pictures, Ltd., London: 102
New York Public Library, Astor, Lenox, and Tilden Foundations, Copy Services: 47, 70; Print Collection, The Miriam and Ira D. Wallach Division of Art, Prints, and Photographs: p. 13, 7, 16, 17, 18, 19, 116 (all Albert E. Gallatin Collection), 87

Philadelphia Museum of Art: 3 (purchased William S. Pilling Fund)
Pierpont Morgan Library, New York: 100 (Bequest of John S. Thatcher, copyright 1994)
Revillon, Inc., New York: 121
Royal Ontario Museum, Toronto (M. Brock Fenton): 27
Professeur Maxime Seligmann, Paris: 75
Sterling and Francine Clark Art Institute, Williamstown, Massachusetts: 109 (copyright 1994)
Tate Gallery, London: 62, 68
Toledo Museum of Art: 131 (purchased with funds from the Libbey Endowment, gift of Edward Drummond Libbey)
U.C.L.A. at The Armand Hammer Museum of Art and Cultural Center, Los Angeles: 54
University of Texas at Austin, Harry Ransom Humanities Research Center, with permission of Dr. Eva Reichmann, Ph.D.: 52
Victoria and Albert Museum, London: 65
Walters Art Gallery, Baltimore: 130
Ed Watkins Photography: 98
Whistler House Museum of Art, Lowell, Massachusetts (Carol Durand): 2
Yale University Library, Beinecke Rare Book and Manuscript Library: 34, 51

To Baronne Elie de Rothschild

All translations from the French are the author's. Montesquiou's poetry, being fundamentally untranslatable, has been left in French whenever cited. Throughout the many citations from Whistler's and his wife's letters, their original spelling and punctuation have been retained.

Contents

Foreword

Exactly ten years ago, Edgar Munhall organized an exhibition at The Frick Collection and wrote a catalogue—really a book—in connection with it devoted to Ingres and the Comtesse d'Haussonville. The focus of the exhibition was the great painting here of the countess by Ingres, and although other institutions before 1985, and many more since then, have held exhibitions around a single work of art, that event remains a milestone for such projects. We were able to present not only a remarkable group of preparatory studies for the portrait, along with other material concerning its evolution and the collaboration of the sitter and the artist over three years, but also memorabilia of the countess and the actual objects shown in the painting, as well as similar clothing. Beyond that, Mr. Munhall studied the sources from which Ingres derived some of his ideas, and then the relationship of the painting to past art and to important works which came afterwards.

Now he has created an equally rich, even more extraordinary story of a painting and of its artist and the subject, two of the most amazing, flamboyant figures in a brilliantly colorful age. This is the saga of James Abbott McNeill Whistler's painting of Comte Robert de Montesquiou-Fezensac. Whistler and Montesquiou were involved in its creation for nearly a decade, from 1885 to 1894. In the beginning of the story we find John Singer Sargent and Henry James, and afterwards the figures include Prince Edmond de Polignac, Comtesse Greffulhe, Marcel Proust, Stéphane Mallarmé, Edmond de Goncourt, Edward Burne-Jones, Paul Helleu, William Morris, Graham Robertson, John Lavery, Camille Pissarro, and Giovanni Boldini. The scene is composed of poets and letter writers as much as painters and printmakers. It is the grandest aristocratic world and the world of upper bohemia: the smart, the fashionable, the raffish, and the witty. It is the most intense expression of the Mauve Decade in France, England, and America.

Swagger portraits and sardonic caricatures fill these pages, as well as delicate landscapes in oil or pastel or lithograph. There are interiors and furniture; above all we find an obsession with clothing. We see the famous Peacock Room, and we see the garments of the most sartorially splendid men, the peacocks of their age. All of these things are described in the pages which follow in words and in dozens of pictures. In many ways this book becomes an illustrated social history of the *fin-de-siècle* salon and studio worlds which often coexisted with that of literature.

We are profoundly grateful to Edgar Munhall, Curator of The Frick Collection, the only begetter of this book and of the exhibition at the Collection (from November 14, 1995, to January 28, 1996) which accompanies its publication. He presents some of the most celebrated works of the late nineteenth century in a fresh and fascinating way; he has also uncovered an impressive amount of unrecognized historical and literary materials, as well as many works of art hitherto little known. He has expressed his debt to the many persons who have helped him in his years of research and writing. I should like to add to his my personal thanks, and the gratitude of the Trustees and staff of The Frick Collection; in particular, I should like to express my own indebtedness to the dedicatee of this book, the Baronne Elie de Rothschild.

Charles Ryskamp
Director
The Frick Collection

Acknowledgments

The earliest epistolary exchange that was to launch this book and the exhibition that will follow it dates back to 1986, but its tone was very hesitant. It was only with the arrival of Charles Ryskamp as Director of The Frick Collection the following year that I knew I had the enthusiastic and committed support I needed. Over the intervening years, other publications, exhibitions, and an audiovisual project have delayed the research toward and the writing of this book, but with the blessings of the Director and of the Trustees of The Frick Collection—to whom I address my first thanks—I was able to devote most of the last three years to a rewarding concentration on Whistler and Montesquiou.

However, without the generous help and sensitive understanding of the Baronne Elie de Rothschild, I could not have gone far. It was she who introduced me to probably the only person alive who remembers Montesquiou—Mme Howard-Johnston, the beautiful Paulette Helleu—and to Comte Armand-Ghislain de Maigret, great-grandson of the Comtesse Greffulhe, who has played such a pivotal role in all that I have managed to do. He in turn presented me to the charming occupant of Whistler's Paris studio—Hortense Damiron—and to a number of young scholars already working in my new field—Anne de Cossé-Brissac, Hélène Dubost-Rouressol, and Antoine Bertrand, whose long-awaited biography of Montesquiou will probably appear soon after this abbreviated one. Bertrand, who knows Montesquiou's life deeply, both in fact and in spirit, has aided me in many important ways.

The amount of archival material Whistler and Montesquiou left behind them is awesome. For someone trying to study it in a hurry, as I had to, expert help was needed. This I readily obtained from my new friends at the Glasgow University Library, which houses the largest collection of Whistler documents in the world. During my brief visits there and subsequently through innumerable calls, faxes, and letters, I experienced nothing but total generosity and attention from Margaret MacDonald, Research Fellow at the Centre for Whistler Studies, and, especially, from Nigel Thorp, Director of the Centre. Timothy Hobbs, Keeper of Special Collections at the Library, and Martin Hopkinson, Curator of the Hunterian Art Gallery, facilitated the photography of important items illustrated in these pages. Finally, Joy Newton, Professor in the French Department at the University of Glasgow, has shared her vast knowledge of Montesquiou's and Whistler's world without restraint, even permitting me to re-use in reverse the title of her edition of the two men's correspondence—*La Chauve-Souris et le papillon*—and to quote from it extensively. I am grateful to the Librarian of the Glasgow University Library for permission to publish here quotations from materials in the Library's Department of Special Collections.

If my contacts in the Département des Manuscrits at the Bibliothèque Nationale de France were less personal, I nevertheless owe a great debt to Mme Florence Callu, *Directeur,* who facilitated my study of the Montesquiou papers preserved there and gave me permission to publish here extensive excerpts from them. Lucien Defaut, *chef des magasiniers,* did his best to keep me constantly supplied with new batches of the boxes containing them.

My peregrinations led me, in fact, to many libraries and archives, and it is a pleasure to acknowledge here the skilled and friendly help I received at the library of the French Institute/Alliance Française in New York, the Frick Art Reference Library, the Library of Congress, the

Lincoln Center Library for the Performing Arts, The New York Public Library, the New York Society Library, and the Thomas J. Watson Library at The Metropolitan Museum of Art, as well as at the Archives of American Art and at those of the Musée Gustave Moreau, supervised by Geneviève Lacambre.

For the first time in my career, I have experienced the luxury of having unpaid volunteers assisting me with my work. Much appreciated were the cheerful and indefatigable efforts of Frédéric Gagnerot-Louis, who contributed so much to the chapter on "The Garb," of Heather Lind, Joanna Serpell, Ashley Thomas, and, most of all, of Manu von Miller, who worked steadily by my side for almost three years. From Paris I received frequent and invaluable assistance from an individual I have yet to meet—Chantal Kensey-Fornacciari.

While a few of my cries for help remain unanswered, it gives me great satisfaction to acknowledge here the special debt I owe each of the following for what they contributed to this project: Vicomte Jacques d'Arjuzon, Paul Audouy, William Ayres, Colin Bailey, Joseph Baillio, Gordon Baldwin, Charles Brock, David S. Brooke, Patrick Cooney, Louis B. Dailey, James Draper, M. Brock Fenton, François Fossier, Vincent Giroud, Alain Goldrach, Maria Hambourg, John Ittmann, William R. Johnston, Katell Le Bourhis, Lamar Lentz, Mark Leonard, Juan José Luna, Barbara Macklowe, Paul G. Marks, Daniel Meyer, Duc and Duchesse de Montesquiou-Fezensac, Claude Potier, Stuart Preston, Hubert Prouté, Jane Rick, Martha Frick Symington Sanger, Rosalind Savill, François-Gérard Seligmann, François Souchal, Elizabeth Streicher, Evan and Brenda Turner, Florence Valdès-Forain, Maïthé Vallès-Bled, the Rev. Edgar Wells, and Michael Wentworth.

I was flattered that Flammarion should publish my book and I am grateful to Suzanne Tise, Director of the Department of English-language Publications, and to her assistant, Diana Groven, for all they have done to see it through completion. The firm's gifted photographer, Frédéric Morellec, skillfully handled a wide variety of subjects and imbued them all with his unique style. Dennis Collins, who has provided a most sensitive translation of my text, helped me in countless other ways with extreme generosity. In New York, my editor was Joseph Focarino; in Paris, Christa Weil. I am indebted to them both.

It was most satisfying to work once again with Nathan Garland, who, in designing this book, deftly managed to create a visual presentation appropriate to its content.

At The Frick Collection I have enjoyed the support of the entire staff, with Robert Goldsmith, Deputy Director for Administration, and Susan Grace Galassi, Assistant Curator, being especially helpful. Our photographer, Richard di Liberto, produced, often in haste, many of the best images reproduced here. William Stout, my assistant and the museum's Registrar, has coped admirably with the myriad details this book and exhibition involved, his good humor always prevailing.

To Richard Barsam and Dylan I address my deepest thanks for supporting me with their affection and endless patience throughout this delightfully obsessive undertaking.

Edgar Munhall
Curator
The Frick Collection

Introduction

> "*Il peint, le maître Whistler,*
> *Le mystère, le mist, l'air.*"
> Robert de Montesquiou [1]

This brief introduction is intended to facilitate the reader's approach to a rather special book.

As its title announces, *Whistler and Montesquiou: The Butterfly and the Bat* is a historical study that focuses on the American expatriate artist James McNeill Whistler (1834–1903) and Comte Robert de Montesquiou-Fezensac (1855–1921), whose portrait Whistler painted in 1891–92. The artist had long before adopted the butterfly as his emblem, seeing in its beautiful uselessness an equivalent to his art. Montesquiou, on the other hand, had early on chosen the bat as his emblem, equating its weirdness with his own bizarre character. The two images recur as *leit-motifs* throughout the book.

At the center of this study is Montesquiou's portrait itself (frontispiece), which has been on public view at The Frick Collection for the last fifty years. Dark and spare, it is often overlooked by casual visitors to the museum, but it caught my eye on the occasion of my first visit as a young man. Already admiring Whistler and having completed my first reading of Proust, I was fascinated to encounter Montesquiou, whom I knew to be one of the models for the unforgettable Baron de Charlus in *A la recherche du temps perdu.*

Many years later, following the success of our 1985 exhibition and book devoted to Ingres' portrait of the *Comtesse d'Haussonville,* also in The Frick Collection, it was natural to consider what other painting here could sustain a similar scrutiny and possibly yield up some of its secrets, as Ingres' had. The choice of Whistler's Montesquiou was easily made.

From the experience of writing an early study I had published on this painting, I knew there was a wealth of documentary material to be utilized. Almost all of the letters Whistler and Montesquiou exchanged had survived, and there was a treasure of other material concerning both men preserved at the Glasgow University Library and the Bibliothèque Nationale de France, as well as in other archives.

The presentation of this material, I decided, would follow the pattern of my study of Ingres' portrait, examining now Montesquiou's, first from one point of view, then from another, and another.

But first, Whistler—the better known of the two protagonists—would be introduced through a summary biography stressing his early and lasting relations with France. He had left his native land by the age of twenty-one, never to return, living mostly in London. But Paris, where he had received his artistic training, constantly beckoned, and Whistler eventually established his studio and residence there in 1892. Through reproductions of some of the many portraits made of him and through contemporary descriptions of his appearance and personality, Whistler could be set at center stage.

Robert de Montesquiou-Fezensac, lesser known, would require a more detailed biography. The scion of a great French family whose origins go back to Merovingian times, Montesquiou had been endowed with traits and talents that often put him at odds with his background, of which he was, all the same, justly proud. Beautiful to behold and extremely bright, abnormally sensitive, industrious, and full of imagination, he realized as a child that he was not like the others and decided to exploit his differences. As he later moved among the highest reaches of Parisian society, he would lash out insolently at those whose social pretensions, intellectual incapacities, or aesthetic shortcomings he scorned. He became a prolific poet of the symbolist caste, a patron and interpreter of the most advanced artists (Gustave Moreau and Émile

M. Menpes, *Five Studies of Whistler* (detail), drypoint, n.d., New York Public Library

A. de La Gandara, *Robert de Montesquiou*, oil on ivory, c. 1875, Paris, Galerie Elstir

Gallé, among others), fashioned himself as a supreme dandy, and created interiors and a life style that complemented his extravagant character. Long before Proust utilized him as a model, Karl Huysmans had done so with the character of des Esseintes in *A rebours,* Jean Lorrain with *Monsieur de Phocas,* Georges Duhamel with the Marquis de Fonfreyde in *Le Désert de Bièvres,* perhaps even, as some believe, Oscar Wilde with *The Picture of Dorian Gray.* Montesquiou was a major celebrity in Paris for the two decades preceeding World War I, as testfied by the many caricatures of him reproduced in this book.

But in addition to recounting the significant adventures of his life, my wish was to evoke the inner man behind his arrogant mask. With frequent references to his memoirs and other writings, quotations from his correspondence, and descriptions penned by his contemporaries, I have attempted to present a man of wildly differing traits, ranging from the demoniac to the childish. It is perhaps among the sad traces of his twenty-year relationship with Gabriel Yturri that we come closest to the real Montesquiou. These two men lived and circulated together, flaunting their love as their ultimate difference, and today they lie buried together in an unmarked tomb.

"The Evolution of the Portrait" is a straightforward account of how Whistler painted his portrait of Montesquiou, from the flirtatious preambles to its commission, through the one hundred torturous sittings, to the painting's final descent from Whistler's studio on its way to its first public showing in 1894.

The excited reactions of Parisians to the portrait open the chapter "The Salon of 1894, and Beyond." Then I follow the painting's history, from Montesquiou's finally taking possession of it that year up to his selling it in 1902 to the colorful American gambler Richard Canfield, who in turn sold it through the Knoedler Gallery to the great collector Henry Clay Frick in 1914.

Because of the portrait's notoriety, people clamored to see reproductions of it. With "The Lithographs," I trace the complicated history of Whistler's own frustrated attempts to duplicate his masterpiece in lithography, and I give here the first detailed account of his wife's efforts to do the same.

Returning to Montesquiou with "The Art Interpreter," I have selected a few of his finest pieces of writing on contemporary art to juxtapose with some remarkable illustrations of works by artists he favored. Including a sampling of paintings, drawings, and prints he owned himself, their range—from Alfred Stevens to Adolphe Monticelli—is startling.

Whistler's portrait is a subtle *hommage* to Montesquiou the dandy. With "The Garb," each element of the clothing represented is analyzed and related to men's fashions of the early 1890s. But since the work is more than a mere fashion plate, I suggest how Whistler contrived to make it convey some of the deeper implications behind Montesquiou's obsession with his appearance.

The final chapter, "The Black Portraits," considers Whistler's formal and other intentions with his portrait of Montesquiou, and its place within the genus of the numerous "Arrangements in Black" the artist painted over the years. Pushing his reductive process to the brink of abstraction, Whistler nevertheless captured and still manages to confront us today with the psychological essence of Robert de Montesquiou. "Look at me for an instant longer," the artist had told the poet, "and you will look forever!"

Whistler First

Whistler's earthly existence has been the subject of many studies, some begun during his lifetime and with his wary encouragement. The major incidents have long been familiar to admirers of the artist and do not require a detailed retelling within the special limits of this book, but the most significant points of reference are nonetheless listed in the following chronology, based on one compiled by Margaret MacDonald.[2] Emphasis has been placed here on Whistler's French connections prior to his beginning the portrait of Robert de Montesquiou in 1891.

Chronology

1834–50. James Abbott Whistler was born in Lowell, Massachusetts (see fig. 2), under the sign of Cancer on July 11, 1834, twenty-one years before Montesquiou. He was the third son of Major George Washington Whistler, a civil engineer, and the eldest son of his second wife, Anna Matilda McNeill. His mother's heritage was Scottish, his father's Irish. In 1843 Mrs. Whistler and her children joined Major Whistler in St. Petersburg, where he was a consulting engineer for the new St. Petersburg-to-Moscow railway. "Jimmy," as he was to be known, had his first art classes at the Imperial Academy of Fine Arts and with an advanced student, Alexander Koritskii. He also must have begun to learn French as a boarder at M. Jourdain's school; he would later speak and write it with perfect ease. In 1849 Whistler went to stay in London with his half-sister Deborah and her husband, Francis Seymour Haden, who would later gain note as an etcher. After Major Whistler's death that April, Mrs. Whistler and James' brother William joined him in England. The family returned to the United States in August.

1851–54. In 1851 Whistler entered The United States Military Academy at West Point. While there, the future artist permanently adopted his mother's maiden name, calling himself James McNeill Whistler, but his fellow cadets knew him as "Curly." His first published work, a lithograph he drew as the cover-page for a music sheet, appeared in 1852. In June 1854 Whistler was discharged from the Academy for deficiency in chemistry, though he was top in his class for drawing. The following November he joined the United States Coast and Geodetic Survey in Washington, etching maps and topographical plans. Though with this work he was essentially reproducing the drawings of others, he did master there the technique of etching. At the time he was described by a colleague as "painfully near-sighted" (hence the later monocle).

1855–59. After painting his first portraits in Baltimore, Whistler set off for Paris to study art. He disembarked at Le Havre on November 2, 1855, aged twenty-one, never to return to his native land. Enrolled at the École Impériale et Spéciale de Dessin, he led a largely carefree bohemian life, frequently changing addresses in the Latin Quarter. His future subject Montesquiou was born in 1855, farther west in the Faubourg Saint-Germain. The following June Whistler entered the tuition-free studio of Charles Gleyre (1808–74). In addition to the inheritance from his father's estate that he had received upon turning twenty-one and an allowance from his family, he got financial support from the American art agent

1 W. M. Chase, *James Abbott
McNeill Whistler,* oil, 1885, New York,
Metropolitan Museum of Art

2 *Whistler's Birthplace in Lowell, Massachusetts,* built in 1831

3 Whistler, *Street in Saverne* from *Douze Eaux-fortes d'après nature,* etching, 1858, Philadelphia Museum of Art

George Lucas, as well as from the Ionides brothers, his first patrons. On commission, Whistler copied paintings in the Louvre and in the Musée du Luxembourg by Boucher, Couture, Greuze, Ingres, Mignard, and others. In 1857 he viewed the Art Treasures exhibition at Manchester, which included fourteen works by or attributed to Velázquez (see fig. 127). Whistler's first major painting, *At the Piano* (Cincinnati, Taft Museum), was rejected by the Salon jury in 1859, but the same exhibition included two etchings from a group he had published the previous year as *Douze Eaux-fortes d'après nature,* since known as "The French Set" (see fig. 3). Among contemporary French artists Whistler came to know Bracquemond, Carolus-Duran, Fantin-Latour, Legros, Tissot, and, most important of all, Courbet. A fellow artist in Paris recorded that "during his humble beginnings in Paris, [Whistler] washed his own clothes, but he was always dressed impeccably." He already had his familiar "aigrette" tuft of white hair amid his curly black locks.

1859–63. In the spring of 1859 Whistler settled in London, where he began "The Thames Set" of etchings, later to be praised by Baudelaire. In 1859 two of these were shown at the Royal Academy, where the following year *At the Piano* was exhibited and sold. Recovering from a bout of the rheumatic fever that plagued him all his life, Whistler spent three months in 1861 painting in Brittany. That winter he executed in Paris *Symphony in White, No. 1: The White Girl* (Washington, National Gallery of Art). Rejected by the Royal Academy in 1862 (provoking the first of Whistler's many letters to the press) and by the Salon jury in Paris the following year, the picture caused a sensation at the Salon des Refusés, along with Manet's *Déjeuner sur l'herbe.* Whistler's reputation as a controversial figure was established.

1864–72. The artist was in Paris in 1864 posing with Manet, Baudelaire, and others for Fantin-Latour's *Hommage à Delacroix* (Paris, Musée d'Orsay), and the following year he exhibited at the Salon his *Princesse du pays de la porcelaine* (Washington, Freer Gallery of Art), a picture that showed his intense interest in Oriental subjects and principles of design. In 1865 he was painting seascapes alongside Courbet at Trouville, but two years later Whistler told Fantin-Latour he wished he had associated with Ingres instead of Courbet. The year 1866 found the artist for six months in Chile, where he painted the *Symphony in Grey and Green: The Ocean* (fig. 5). In April 1867 Whistler pushed his brother-in-law Haden through a plate-glass window in Paris in a dispute over the latter's treatment of a colleague. The following month four of Whistler's paintings were exhibited at the Exposition Universelle. By 1869 Whistler ceased signing his work with his name, using instead the now-familar butterfly insignia based on his initials JW. Unlike Montesquiou's chosen emblems, the bat and the blue hydrangea, Whistler's butterfly had cheerful, even carefree associations, for most people assume the sole purpose of the butterfly's existence is to delight with its beauty—a perfect parallel to Whistler's aesthetic credo. But often Whistler appended a stinging, scorpion's tail to his butterflies, alluding to the less playful side of his character (fig. 6). Just as Montesquiou collected real bats, so did Whistler collect mounted butterflies (fig. 8). He also used their images to adorn the case that

4 Whistler, *Portrait of the Artist,* black and white chalk, 1860s, Washington, Freer Gallery of Art

contained his calling cards (fig. 9) and signed much of his correspondence with a butterfly. During the spring of 1871 the artist published his *Sixteen Etchings of Scenes on the Thames* and began to paint his series of night scenes along the river, which he later called "Nocturnes." That summer he executed his most famous work, *Arrangement in Grey and Black: Portrait of the Painter's Mother* (fig. 10). The portrait was shown at the Royal Academy in 1872, but only after being initially rejected. Whistler never exhibited with the institution again.

1873–79. In 1873, the artist's self-portrait *Arrangement in Grey: Portrait of the Painter* (Detroit Institute of Arts) and several Thames views were shown at the Galerie Durand-Ruel in Paris. During the summer of 1876 Whistler worked on the decoration of the dining room at Frederick Leyland's London residence (fig. 11). Annoyed with the artist's vastly exceeding what he was to have done and by the attendant publicity over the Peacock Room, Leyland paid Whistler only half of what he had expected. This trauma was followed in May 1877 by John Ruskin's writing, in reference to *Nocturne in Black and Gold: The Falling Rocket* (Detroit Institute of Arts), that he had "never expected to hear a coxcomb ask two hundred guineas for flinging a pot of paint in the public's face." Whistler sued Ruskin for libel. At the trial in November of 1878, the artist was awarded a farthing's damage without costs. Now in desperate financial straits, Whistler was declared bankrupt on May 8, 1879. Just prior, an auction sale of his paintings, etchings, drawings, porcelain, and household effects was held at Whistler's London home, the White House. The following September the artist set out for Venice with a commission from the Fine Art Society to execute twelve etchings.

1880–85. By May of 1880 Whistler had executed fifty etchings and over sixty pastels in Venice (cf. fig. 12). Immediately upon returning to London in late 1880, he exhibited twelve of the etchings, known as "The First Venice Set" (cf. fig. 13), and the following January he showed a large group of pastels. At the Salon of 1882 the artist exhibited his portrait of *Lady Meux* (New York, The Frick Collection) and three Venetian etchings. The next year he showed the portrait of his mother; it was awarded a third-class medal and was reviewed enthusiastically by Théodore Duret, to whom Manet had introduced Whistler and whose portrait Whistler painted shortly afterward (fig. 115). Duret would publish his definitive *Histoire de J. McN. Whistler et de son oeuvre* in 1904. In 1883 Whistler was also exhibiting Nocturnes at the Galerie Georges Petit. On February 20, 1885, in Princes Hall, he delivered the "Ten O'Clock" lecture, setting forth his artistic principles. On July 3 Whistler encountered Montesquiou for the first time over dinner at the Reform Club with Henry James. In August Whistler travelled in Belgium and the Netherlands with William Merritt Chase, who painted his portrait in a Whistlerian manner (fig. 1). The following month he was visiting the English art colony in Dieppe.

1886–90. The portrait of Sarasate (fig. 124) appeared at the Salon of 1886. In 1887 a large group of oils, watercolors, and pastels by Whistler was shown at the Exposition Internationale de Peinture in Paris. Still more were on view at the Galerie Durand-Ruel the following year. That June

5 Whistler, *Symphony in Grey and Green: The Ocean,* oil, 1866, New York, Frick Collection

Monet introduced Whistler to Mallarmé (fig. 14), who would become a close friend, a frequent correspondent, and the translator of the "Ten O'Clock" lecture. On August 11 the artist married Beatrice Godwin, widow of the architect E. W. Godwin. They spent a working honeymoon in France through November. A banquet honoring Whistler was held in Paris in April 1889. The artist won a gold medal at the Exposition Universelle that year, and was named a Chevalier of the Légion d'Honneur. In March of 1890 he met C. L. Freer of Detroit, who would form a major collection of his work, now in Washington. *The Gentle Art of Making Enemies* was published that June.

1891–94. Whistler worked on Montesquiou's portrait in 1891 and 1892, and then kept it in his studio for two years. The Corporation of Glasgow in April 1891 bought Whistler's portrait of Carlyle, the first of his paintings to be acquired for a public collection. That same year the artist ceased exhibiting at the Salon of the Société des Artistes Français in favor of the more progressive one of the Société Nationale des Beaux-Arts. In November Whistler's portrait of his mother was acquired for the Musée du Luxembourg (the state museum for contemporary art), and the following January the artist was elevated to Officier of the Légion d'Honneur. The Duc d'Aumale invited Whistler and Montesquiou for luncheon at the château of Chantilly in late June, an event noted in the press. Whistler and his wife settled into their new Paris residence at 110 rue du Bac in September 1892; the artist had a separate studio at 86 rue Notre-Dame-des-Champs. The couple visited Brittany the following

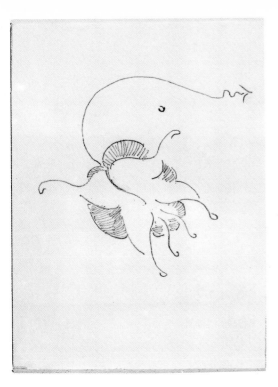

7 W. Crane, *Whistler as a Butterfly*,
pen and ink wash, n.d.,
New York Public Library

6 Whistler, *The Artist's Butterfly*,
pencil, n.d., New York, Metropolitan
Museum of Art

8 *Morpho Cypris Butterfly owned by Whistler*,
Glasgow, Hunterian Art Gallery

9 French, *Whistler's Calling-Card Case*, leather,
c. 1892, Glasgow, Hunterian Art Gallery

summer. Montesquiou's portrait appeared at the Salon of the Champ-de-Mars in April 1894, provoking a generally enthusiastic response.

1895–1905. Whistler was troubled throughout the year 1895 by Beatrice's declining health. She died of cancer on May 10, 1896. He adopted his sister-in-law Rosalind Birnie Philip as his ward, and made her his executrix. That summer he spent some time painting around Dieppe and Calais. The opening in November of the first annual exhibition at The Carnegie Institute, Pittsburgh, featured the portrait of Sarasate (fig. 124), recently acquired by that institution. Whistler sat for his own portrait by Boldini (fig. 15) in 1897, looking remarkably alert, though Boldini also did a drypoint showing Whistler dozing after lunch (fig. 16). In September of 1898 Mallarmé's death considerably upset Whistler, who was ill himself. That fall he became involved in directing the Académie Carmen in Paris, founded by a former model of his, Carmen Rossi. In April 1900, at the request of the American Commissioner, he showed *The Little White Girl* and other works at the Exposition Universelle, where he was awarded a separate Grand Prix for his paintings and etchings. Whistler was elected an honorary member of the Académie des Beaux-Arts in 1901. Later that year he closed his Paris studio and sold the apartment in the rue du Bac. In 1902 the artist first met Richard A. Canfield, who would assemble a major Whistler collection, including the portrait of Montesquiou which he purchased in October of that year. On August 3, 1902, Whistler wrote to the *Morning Post,* congratulating them on publishing his obituary prematurely. The University of Glasgow awarded him an honorary degree of Doctor of Laws in April 1903. Whistler died on July 17 of that year and was buried in Chiswick Cemetery. His pallbearers were Théodore Duret, Sir James Guthrie, John Lavery, Edwin A. Abbey, George Vanderbilt, and C. L. Freer. Before the funeral, both Joanna Hiffernan and Maud Franklin, former lovers of Whistler, had come to view him in his studio. Over four hundred works by Whistler were shown in the 1905 memorial exhibition held at the École des Beaux-Arts, *Oeuvres de James McNeill Whistler.*

In appearance and personality, Whistler stood out from the crowd and made every effort to do so. He was endowed by nature with good looks and inexhaustible energy. Though small (he was called a "pocket Apollo" in his youth), he had a vigorous physique that impressed his printers as he manipulated the powerful lithographic presses.

Unlike Montesquiou, Whistler appears to have been resolutely heterosexual. Though a colleague of his at the United States Coast Survey recalled that he "was not interested in young ladies," [2] during his student days in Paris his models had a way of becoming his mistresses. Later, living in London, the artist had prolonged liaisons with two women: Joanna Hiffernan, the beautiful Irish model who posed for *The White Girl* and who was immortalized as Courbet's *La Belle irlandaise;* and Maud Franklin, a feisty model Whistler once memorably referred to as an "obscure nobody." The first relationship lasted from 1860 to 1866; the second, from about 1872 until Whistler's marriage to Beatrice Godwin in 1888. Both women were redheads. With Maud Franklin, who was less than half his age, Whistler had at least two daughters: Ióne, born probably in 1877, and Maud McNeill Whistler Franklin, so registered by her

10 Whistler, *Arrangement in Grey and Black: Portrait of the Painter's Mother,* oil, 1871, Paris, Musée d'Orsay

11 Whistler, *Harmony in Blue and Gold: The Peacock Room* (southeast corner), oil and gold leaf, 1876–77, Washington, Freer Gallery of Art

12 Whistler, *Nocturne—The Riva,* pastel, 1879–80, New York, Frick Collection

mother as born on February 13, 1879. The father's name was not listed. Maud probably had at least one more pregnancy that produced a child who died in infancy.[3] She herself lived on until 1941. In addition to these rather complex relationships, in 1870 Whistler fathered a son, Charles James Whistler Hanson, with Louisa Hanson, a parlormaid. He was also briefly engaged in 1872 to Mrs. Leyland's sister, Elizabeth Dawson.

Descriptions

There remain many vivid descriptions of Whistler by his contemporaries. A brief selection of some of the less familiar ones follows:

> John Ross Key, 1854: "I do not recall his making any intimate friendships with those whom we met either at the billiard room or in the office.…He had no bad habits, and did not smoke. His manners were quiet and sedate, and his attractive personality interested every one with whom he came in contact, and I never knew any one to say an unkind word of him." [4]

> Louisine Havemeyer, 1874: "Whistler entered almost immediately. Instantly I felt a flash as I looked at him and an impression was printed forever indelibly upon my memory.…He was a black Loge against the yellow light.…Loge the fire god, restless, excitable, with a burning intelligence concentrated in his piercing black eyes, a personality with a power to focus itself beyond

13 Whistler, *Nocturne,* etching, 1879,
New York, Frick Collection

resistance, a power that enjoyed the shock it produced, and a gay
spontaneous irreverence. He certainly was a Loge incarnate,
a fire who emitted the sparks he swallowed and laughed as the
shower fell upon the public whom he held in such contempt.
I assure you I was thrilled as I shook his hand and felt at once
that I could anticipate a new experience. Strange to say I
immediately was at ease and had no fear of him whatever." [5]

Graham Robertson (fig. 68), 1890: "But…instead of the Whistler
of legend entered a wholly delightful personage, an *homme du
monde* whose old-world courtesy smoothed away all awkwardness
and who exercised an almost hypnotic fascination such as I have
met with in no one else. I knew him for Whistler by the restless
vitality of the dark eyes; there was the dapper figure, the black
curls, the far-famed white lock, but of the scoffer, the Papilio
mordens, not a trace. We seemed to slip into a sudden intimacy.
…The first impression of a friendly Whistler was, I am glad to
say, never effaced.…The man whom I knew was courteous,
kindly and affectionate and showed a lovable side to his nature
with which he is not often credited." [6]

Léon Daudet, c. 1890: "His laugh was even more singular than
his features, set and worn by sarcasm, and was composed of
two or three laughs, each of a different tone, imbued, one with
surprise, another with acerbic irony, and the third with the

14 Whistler, *Portrait of Stéphane Mallarmé,* drypoint, c. 1890, Glasgow, Hunterian Art Gallery

15 G. Boldini, *Portrait of James McNeill Whistler,* oil, 1897, Brooklyn Museum

16 G. Boldini, *Whistler Asleep on a Sofa,*
drypoint, 1897, New York Public Library

17 M. Menpes, *Whistler Laughing,*
drypoint, 1884–86, New York Public
Library

18 Dornac, *Whistler in his Studio, rue Notre-Dame-des-Champs,* albumen photoprint, after 1892, New York Public Library

19 P. Helleu, *Portrait of Whistler*, drypoint, 1897, New York Public Library

20 M. Beerbohm, *Mr Whistler*, graphite and ink, n.d., Cambridge, Massachusetts, Houghton Library, Harvard University

egotistical pleasure that came from having his point understood. These three laughs taken together announced the precious demon miles away. Everyone one would exclaim: 'It's Whistler!'" [7]

Arthur Symons, 1890s: "I remember the first dinner party at which I first met him…there was a sharp crackle from Whistler's corner, and it was as if a rattlesnake had leapt suddenly out.… All his laughter was a crackling of thorns under the pot, but of flaming thorns, setting the pot in a fury of boiling. I never saw any one so feverishly alive as this little, old man, with his bright, withered cheeks, over which the skin was drawn tightly, his darting eyes, under their prickly bushes of eyebrow, his fantastically creased black and white curls of hair, his bitter and subtle mouth, and above all, his exquisite hands, never at rest. He had the most sensitive fingers I have ever seen, long, thin, bony, wrinkled, every finger alive to the tips, like the fingers of a mesmerist. He was proud of his hands, and they were never out of sight; they travelled to his moustache, crawled over the table, grimaced in little gestures. If ever a painter had painter's hands it was Whistler. And his voice, with its strange accent, part American, part deliberately French, part tuned to the key of his wit, was not less personal or significant." [8]

John Lavery, after 1897: "When he got in front of the glass to brush his hair he behaved exactly like a woman settling her permanent wave, placing individual locks, moistened to keep their form, in their allotted places so that they did not interfere with the grey wisp of which he was so proud that stood out of the damp shiny curls on his forehead. His eyebrows were thick and black, his eyes sharp as needles, while a sensitive nose and mouth with prominent chin made up his features. He had beautiful hands, though somewhat clawlike, especially when he would clutch one by the arm to drive home a point. A low, turn-down collar with a narrow black-ribbon bow adorned his wrinkled neck, and his general appearance was that of a small alert ringmaster, whip in hand. I can never remember seeing him, even in the country, in anything other than what are known as court slippers, causing him to be very careful where he stepped out of doors." [9]

Walter Gay, 1903: "I went to see him in London, a short time before he died. It was a very touching visit; he was so glad to see me, but we both knew that we were not to meet again and that the end was near. I remember he would not let me go, but held on to my hand. I sat down with him again, and he still held my hand. I had to tear myself away finally." [10]

Montesquiou

What Montesquiou would one day call his "future corpse" first saw the light of day at eleven o'clock in the morning on March 19, 1855, in his grandfather's Paris residence, the Hôtel de Béthune, still standing today at 60 rue de Varenne (fig. 22). His parents occupied an apartment on the third floor. This Piscean child would later describe the drama of his birth so: "…the mother shrieks, the child lets out a cry, and these two voices respond to one another, the one complaining at having given life, the other lamenting for having received it!" [1] The boy, named Marie-Joseph-Anatole-Robert de Montesquiou-Fezensac, was baptized on March 21.

His mother, Albertine-Marie-Pauline Duroux (1823–64), was born in Paris, though her son would insist she was Swiss. Pauline was ugly, Protestant, bourgeois, and very rich. She had previously given birth to a daughter, Élise (1845–79), and two sons, Gontran (1847–83) and Aimery (1853–73).

The future poet's father, Comte Thierry de Montesquiou-Fezensac (1824–1904), descended from a great French family that traces its origins back to the Merovingian kings (c. 500–750). It issued from the counts of Fezensac, of whom the first Comte Aimery lived at the beginning of the eleventh century. The Montesquious joined the line soon after. Over the centuries the family produced such notable figures as: Blaise de Montluc (1501–77), Maréchal de France, who served under four French kings and left behind his *Commentaires,* dubbed "the soldier's Bible" by Henri IV; François de Montesquiou, Maréchal de Gassion, one of the rare friends the same monarch addressed as "*tu*"; Jean de Montluc, the humanist Bishop of Valence; and, the best known of all the family's military forebears, Charles de Baatz de Castelmore (1611–73), Seigneur d'Artagnan, Captain of the Royal Musketeers under Louis XIV, whose pseudo-memoirs were the inspiration for Dumas' *The Three Musketeers*. In 1905 Robert de Montesquiou would take great pride in assuring the readers of *Le Figaro* that a real d'Artagnan had in fact once existed. He addressed his letter from the Château d'Artagnan in the Hautes-Pyrénées, a property that had belonged to the Montesquious since 1608 but which Robert felt compelled to sell in 1920. In his memoirs, no doubt reflecting bitterly upon his own recent literary reincarnation as Proust's Baron de Charlus, he pondered the case of his ancestor: "Is it admissable, is it desirable to see a fictional character overtake its model, to the point of relegating him to the background and almost replacing him in people's memories?" [2]

Another d'Artagnan, Pierre de Montesquiou (1640–1725), was Maréchal de France during the last years of Louis XIV. Saint-Simon and others recorded that he was responsible for the crucial French victory at Denain during the War of the Spanish Succession, though ever afterward the Maréchal de Villars, Montesquiou's superior officer, has been credited for this, much to Robert's smoldering indignation. Next to achieve fame for the family was Anne-Pierre de Montesquiou, Marquis de Fezensac (1739–98). Also a military man, he was named Maréchal-de-camp in 1780. At the same time his talents as a poet and playwright brought him election to the Académie Française, an honor some thought his nine-teenth-century descendant merited. This marquis took a liberal turn during the Revolution. Though his fellow nobles elected him deputy to the States General, he joined the Third Estate. As Commander-in-Chief,

21 L. Doucet, *Portrait of Comte Robert de Montesquiou-Fezensac,* oil, 1879, Musée et Domaine National de Versailles, bequest of Robert de Montesquiou

22 *Entrance Portal of the Hôtel de Béthune, 60 rue de Varenne, Paris,* photographed in 1993

23 F. Morellec, *Façade of 41 quai d'Orsay, Paris,* photographed in 1994

24 J. Bastien-Lepage, *Portrait of Robert de Montesquiou,* pen and ink wash, 1879, Paris, private collection

he completed the conquest of Savoy in 1792.

The family's most remarkable figure in recent times was Robert's great-grandmother, Comtesse Louise-Charlotte-Françoise de Montesquiou-Fezensac (d. 1835), chosen by Napoleon to be the governess of his son, the King of Rome. Her charge called her "*Maman Quiou,*" and the Emperor wrote of her with fervor: "She is a woman of rare excellence; her piety is sincere, her principles excellent; she has earned great titles in my esteem and in my affection. I could have used two like her, half a dozen; I should have placed all of them with distinction, and I should have asked for still more." [3] With her immense fortune, she brought the château of Courtenvaux into the family and, more specifically for Robert's immediate benefit, the layette of the King of Rome, which she had been given at the end of her imperial services. Her great-grandson recalled wearing as an infant these embroidered and lace-festooned garments. From this ancestor the future poet inherited as well the Empire bed he would present to Whistler one day (fig. 65). This countess' son Anatole-Ambroise-Augustin (1788–1878)—Robert's grandfather—served as aide-de-camp to Napoleon I, but was also a poet (of the "automatic school," according to his grandson) and author of memoirs. He married his first cousin, Germaine-Élodie de Montesquiou-Fezensac. Like his grandson, he was attracted by the occult and was apparently a successful medium. [4] Robert believed that it was with these sensibilities that he perceived the special qualities of his favorite grandchild.

Thierry de Montesquiou had sought to follow in the diplomatic tradition of his family, gaining an appointment to the Ministry of Foreign

25 Unknown photographer, *Ground-floor Salon, Pavillon Montesquiou, Versailles,* from *La Revue illustrée,* August 1, 1894, Washington, Library of Congress

Affairs, but he gave up that post soon after his marriage in 1844 in order to look after his newly acquired wealth. With Pauline's dowry Thierry purchased a château in the Loire Valley, Charnizay, in a locale later described by his son as "the only spot in the Touraine that is not beautiful." [5] In 1863 he also undertook the construction, along with a cousin, of a large hôtel at the corner of the quai d'Orsay and the boulevard de la Tour Maubourg. Still standing, this residence is ornamented on its façade with the Montesquiou arms and initials (fig. 23).

His youngest son was fortunate in coming by his father's height and good looks, but Robert was never inclined to follow Thierry's avaricious habits. Son and father in fact had little in common. This tight-fisted vice president of the Jockey Club was soon recognized by Robert as lacking any esthetic sense, and so there was "an *initial antagonism,* that never ceased…an inexorable veto of any possible relationship between us." [6] Their most poignant exchange occurred in a twisting staircase at Charnizay. Stung by his father's criticisms, Robert cried out, "You should have made me differently!"—to which his father responded, "I didn't do it on purpose." [7]

The Comtesse Thierry de Montesquiou loved her husband absolutely, to the detriment of her children. Converted to Catholicism, she devoted herself to her charities and to work on an endless panel of embroidery destined to cover a suite of furniture in the salon. Its recurring motif was a garland of hydrangeas, the plant that would later obsess her youngest child. The countess died in 1864, aged forty-one. Her three eldest children soon followed, in 1873, 1879, and 1883, leaving only Robert

26 Unknown photographer,
*Montesquiou's Bedroom, Pavillon
Montesquiou, Versailles,* from *La Revue
illustrée,* August 1, 1894, Washington,
Library of Congress

and his father face to face.

Tutors had been hired early on to train Gontran, Aimery, and
Robert. Rather than getting the Erasmus the latter dreamed of, their
father engaged a M. Keller, whom his youngest pupil remembered as
"brutal, coarse, unintelligent, arbitrary, and acrimonious." [8] With another
tutor, Robert engaged in poetic combats, prefiguring the dazzling
performance he gave at his *baccalauréat* examination, rendering in French
verse his translation of the assigned Latin poem.

Of all the individuals in his early life who marked Robert in one
way or another, the most significant was Marguerite Loiseau, a servant.
Taken on as a girl by the recently married Montesquious in the mid 1840s,
she remained with the family until her death (in 1891, when Robert was
posing for Whistler). For this woman Robert felt and recorded a deep
affection that seems unique in his life, referring to her in his memoirs as
"the sole being of whom I can write here with tenderness, with filial piety,
with gratitude, for she was truly the one I should call my mother." [9]
Marguerite Loiseau attended the Comtesse de Montesquiou at her death,
as well as the twenty-year-old Aimery at his, and Robert did the same
for this servant, burying her with his own hands. He carefully preserved
the letters he had received from Marguerite, justly praising their style. An
example is the following passage taken from a note of condolence the
servant addressed her master upon the death of his grandmother:

As you say, my dear child, what a change this is going to make
everywhere, especially at poor Courtenvaux, of which it can be
said that once it was Paradise on earth. Everyone lived there

27 Chinese, *Robe* (detail), embroidered
silk, Ch'ing dynasty, Toronto, Royal
Ontario Museum

content; masters and servants came together as one family; the
former trying to keep us together with our husbands and
children, so that we might be happy among ourselves, and we
sought, through our devotion, to demonstrate our gratitude.[10]

Robert was devoted to the memory of Marguerite Loiseau not
only for herself, but also because he associated her nostalgically with the
cloudless period of his childhood spent at Courtenvaux, evoked so simply
in the stanzas of "Ancilla" published in *Les Hortensias bleus* in 1896:

> *Hélas! que j'ai trouvé tristes et solennelles*
> *Les heures qui pour moi, sonnaient avec ta fin*
> *L'irrémissible fin des choses maternelles.*
> *O pauvre Marguerite, O la chère servante,*
> *Âme primordiale et coeur si simple! adieu.*[11]

Around 1865 the Comte de Montesquiou enrolled his son as a
day student at the Lycée Bonaparte (now Lycée Condorcet), on the rue du
Havre—the first of what the boy would call his "prisons." Apparently
unappreciated by his teachers, whom he in turn denigrated, Robert
focused his attention on an older boy in his class who was handsome,
svelte, well dressed, and usually sound asleep.

After two years of this, Robert was transferred to a Jesuit school,
the Collège de l'Immaculée Conception, rue de Vaugirard, where he
remained as a boarder or "inmate" until 1872. Once again he judged his
instructors unacceptable and his fellow students worse. Refusing to
participate in their rough-and-tumble games, declining to address them as
"tu," and withdrawing into a melancholy solitude, Robert later recalled

28 A. Dürer, *Melencolia I* (detail), engraving, 1514, New York, Frick Collection

29 Unknown photographer, *Montesquiou, in Bat-decorated Cloak, with the Comtesse de Montebello at a Costume Ball*, n.d., Paris, private collection

that he was unconsciously conforming to Stendhal's description of one of his characters—"He couldn't please, he was *too different*"— and, without knowing the source, adopting Baudelaire's principle of the "aristocratic pleasure of displeasing."[12] He was cautious in school of the dangers associated with "special friendships," which could lead to the silent disappearance of the guilty parties, and instead threw himself into a frenzy of poetic composition: "hexameters, pentameters, Asclepiad lines."[13] But even these efforts were sometimes pilfered from his desk and made the subject of mockery. Montesquiou later revealed to his idol Edmond de Goncourt (1822–96) that, as a result, he had tended to withdraw into his own world and "carefully hide [within his soul] all tenderness and rapturous emotion."[14]

With his diploma in hand, the seventeen-year-old young man was then assigned by his father to a M. Dufailly for a year's unsuccessful coaching in mathematics. After that, Robert dutifully presented himself as a candidate for military service but was rejected for being "excessively thin." Finally free, he settled down to an existence devoted to what the caricaturist Cham even then characterized as "vagrancy."

Gradually taking over the quai d'Orsay's attic apartment, which had been allotted to his grandmother's resident chaplain, the Abbé Papillon, young Montesquiou began in the mid 1870s to give himself over there to his "love of things" and their installation in "ornamental compositions."[15] Breaking through walls, opening doors and hallways, installing a winding staircase, covering surfaces with decorated leathers and satin, he created out of these low-ceilinged, small rooms the "cavern

30 Montesquiou, *Blue Hydrangeas,* pastel, n.d., Paris, private collection

of an Arabian tale," which he described as being "this mirror of [my] soul at the time." [16] The revelation of contemporary Japanese artifacts at the Exposition Universelle of 1878 led the budding poet to acquire quantities of these at the close of the exhibition, where they had failed to seduce the general public. To do all this took a lot of the young man's money, so he had to turn to his father and convince him of the advisability of selling jewels he had been holding in store for his son's eventual marriage. Robert, however, was already fiercely determined to avoid "that form of captivity." [17]

From the description of this apartment given in Montesquiou's memoirs, it seems to have comprised a salon, library, dining room, boudoir, bedroom, and bath, as well as a sham chapel. The poet lived here some fifteen years, until 1888. Fortunately, he indulged in the luxury of having these rooms photographed,[18] and we can see that certain elements of his first interior reappear in later ones, such as his bronze Japanese bats (fig. 25) or his low "chimera" bed, which he had fashioned out of fragments of Chinese carvings (fig. 26). Of all the evocations of these rooms, none seems so accurate as the one written by Montesquiou's English friend Graham Robertson (see fig. 68):

> It was curious to leave the stately, almost austere rooms of the old Comte and to climb up a dark stairway, through tunnels of tapestry to the eyrie which Comte Robert had elected to inhabit, and to come into the exotic atmosphere of his extraordinary rooms, like a vague dream of the Arabian Nights translated into Japanese: the room of all shades of red, one wall deep crimson, the next rose colour, the third paler rose, and the last the faintest almond pink; the grey room where all was grey and for which he used to ransack Paris weekly to find grey flowers; the bedroom, where a black dragon was apparently waddling away with the bed on his back, carrying the pillow in a coil of his tail and peering out at the foot with glassy, rolling eyes; the bathroom, where one gazed through filmy gauzes painted with fish into a green gloom that might have been "full fathoms five" under waves. It was all queer, disturbing, baroque, yet individual and even beautiful, and as a transmutation of a set of unpromising attics into a tiny fairy palace, little short of a conjuring trick.[19]

Montesquiou claimed to have admitted few visitors to his "cave of Ali Baba," but one individual he did invite there after a dinner around 1882 was the poet Stéphane Mallarmé (1842–98), whom he had known for some time. According to Robert, the older poet "left my apartment in a state of cold exaltation, as was his wont, though it did not frequently rise to this temperature." [20] Mallarmé in turn gave a description of what he had seen to a younger writer, then unknown, Joris Karl Huysmans (1848–1907). The latter adapted what he had learned about Montesquiou and his apartment to create the character of the Duc Jean Floressas des Esseintes, the hero of his novel *A rebours,* which appeared in 1884. The florid decadence of this work, replete with such real Montesquiouian details as the church hand bell serving as a doorbell, the re-use of ecclesiastical architectural elements in a private dwelling, and the turtle whose shell had been gilded and incrusted with jewels, titillated the public, who soon came to learn the identity of the real des Esseintes. Thus for the first of several occasions Montesquiou found himself transposed into a character of fiction. Not acquainted personally with Huysmans, though admiring his work, the young poet objected strenuously to the latter's attributing moral defects and even crimes to his fictional character that Montesquiou felt readers in the know would spontaneously attribute to him as well. Unfortunately the association has stuck, even though such a figure as Edmond de Goncourt defended Montesquiou against it, as in his diary, which reads:

> Montesquiou is not at all the des Esseintes of Huysmans. Even though there is a little *craziness* about him, the gentleman is never caricatural, he always saves himself by his distinction. As for his conversation, aside from a slightly mannered expression, it is full of sharp observations, of delicate remarks, of original observations, of pretty phrases all his own, and which he often concludes by finishing off with a smile in his eye, with nervous gestures of his fingertips.[21]

It was during these same years in the quai d'Orsay house that Montesquiou adopted as his personal emblems the bat and the blue hydrangea. "The bird with wings of skin," as Pliny described the former, caught the poet's attention probably through its many appearances on Oriental lacquer, textiles, jades, and bronzes, where the motif signified happiness and longevity (fig. 27), but he was also aware of its crucial presence and darker significance in Dürer's *Melencolia I* (fig. 28). There the bat signifies the dusk proper to melancholy. Elsewhere this flying mammal has been regarded, among other things, as the first animal in creation, the result of an incestuous and homosexual union between the solar lord and his son. The bat has been associated with the impure, the libidinous, the androgynous, the accursed—all qualities that the sensitive youth may have associated with himself.[22] Later Montesquiou kept a real bat, a long-eared myotis (*Myotis evotis*), in a lacquer cage, "whose delicacy," he recalled, "rendered it so precious, and whose half-shadows gave such melancholic majesty to its tiara-ornamented head that we had come to consider it a metempsychosis of Ludwig II of Bavaria."[23] Finally, no one has yet pointed out that Montesquiou resembled a bat himself, with his winged, upturned moustache and his enormous pointed ears.

The blue hydrangea (*Hydrangea hortensia*), which derives its strange but perfectly natural coloring from sundry agents in the soil, was a more banal discovery at some Parisian florist's, where it made its first appearance during the 1880s. Like most of the decorative bats that Montesquiou had seen, its origins were Chinese and Japanese. Robert's prodigal use of the flower in his interiors and the frequent references he made to it in his poetry and in his drawings (fig. 30) contributed to the blue hydrangea's peculiar popularity over the next decade. The apparent unnaturalness of the flower obviously appealed to Robert, who saw himself always as a being apart from others. The bat and the blue hydrangea taken together—as in Helleu's pastel *Blue Hydrangeas and Bats* (fig. 102), which once belonged to Montesquiou—summed up the poet's whole morbid being, as he explained:

> I felt that this refractory plant associated with this rebellious bird would dominate my life, because the two together would make use of me, to extract, for the one, in its abnormal azure blue, and

31 Montesquiou, *Montesquiou as the Head of John the Baptist,* photoprint and watercolor, c. 1886, Paris, private collection

32 Unknown photographer, *Garden Façade of 8 rue Franklin*, n.d., Musée Clemenceau, Paris

the other, in its colorless anxiety, the thousand and one, perhaps even the thousand and three reasons why they had been designated, among all others, and for ever and ever, to represent the double sign of the joining of *Dissimilarity* and of *Melancholy*....
I am approaching my own twilight, an hour when, more than ever, the company of the winged creature of dusk is appropriate, as well as that of the flower on which the moonlight lingers.
...And all about these troubling clusters would continue the wheeling flight of my "grey sisters" until the moment has come, for the one, to shed its petals, and for the others, to scatter about the last scene of action of their gardener and of their shepherd.[24]

On a more mundane level, Montesquiou cited the significance of the blue hydrangea in the traditional "language of flowers" as being, through its abundance of ornaments, a symbol of coquetry—an appropriate allusion, he conceded, to the overwrought style of his existence and of his literary compositions, to say nothing of his handwriting!

After the death of the Comtesse Gontran de Montesquiou in 1887 (her husband had died four years before), Robert's father began to find the quai d'Orsay house too big and empty and decided to move with his orphaned granddaughter Marie-Aude (b. 1882) to an apartment just across the Seine on the place François-Ier. His son took advantage of this move to set up his own apartment at 8 rue Franklin, just off the present place du Trocadéro. It was from this dwelling he called "the Chelsea of Paris" that Robert would have set out for his posing sessions with Whistler; it was here that Hata the Japanese gardener cultivated the bonsais that Montesquiou presented to the artist; and it was here that Whistler was entertained on numerous occasions, such as the one he described to his wife on June 14, 1891: "A note from Montesquiou—and today passed with him—breakfast! and garden & Japonese tree—and endless talk—and everything charming....He missed you greatly at his little coquetish entertainment this morning."[25]

While he found his father's new abode "tiny, uncomfortable, dark,"[26] Robert was delighted with his own, as he noted in his memoirs:

33 Otto (Wegener), *Portrait of Robert de Montesquiou*, photocard, before 1888, Glasgow University Library

A ground-floor apartment, not exactly immense, but very agreeable, between a courtyard and a garden; the latter, one of four or five into which the big, high wall of ivy joining the Trocadéro to Passy is divided. Thus on a level with the street, on the entrance side, the apartment faced, on the other, a very pleasant enclosure. ...Nothing more than two little salons, a bedroom, a bath and dressing room, a dining room, an entry hall, and a few service areas, but the whole laid out harmoniously; outside, I had a beautiful chestnut tree, outlining itself against a broad expanse of sky, which allowed one to feel far away from Paris.[27]

In July 1891 Edmond de Goncourt visited the apartment, his sharp eye not missing a thing, as he recorded in his journal:

Visit to Montesquiou-Fezensac....A street-level apartment on the rue Franklin, opened up with tall windows set with tiny seventeenth-century panes, giving the house an air of antiquity. A dwelling full of a mishmash of disparate objects, old family portraits, horrible Empire furniture, Japanese *kakémonos*, Whistler etchings....One original room...where the hydrangea is

34 Unknown photographer, *Portrait of Gabriel Yturri*, c. 1904, reproduced from Montesquiou, *Le Chancelier de fleurs*, New Haven, Connecticut, Beinecke Rare Book and Manuscript Library

35 A. de La Gandara, *Gabriel Yturri Reading*, chalk, 1891, Paris, private collection

represented in every medium, and in every manner of painting and drawing. And in the middle of this bath and dressing room, a small mirrored showcase, revealing the tender nuances of a hundred cravates, beneath a slightly pederastic photograph of Larochefoucauld, the gymnast of the Molier circus, wearing tights that show off the pretty forms of this ephebe.[28]

The press too were admitted. Their articles noted that Montesquiou's favorite emblems dominated the new décor, as in these comments:

> Then here a Japanese room with his collection of bats in many forms…the lily-like and deliciously sweet hydrangea is, as we know, the preferred flower of the poet who has equally devoted a sort of cult to the shadowy bat. The strange beast, friend of the shadow and of pale moonlight, and the flower with light tones of apotheosis fill the artistic residence of the Comte de Montesquiou-Fezensac. They are everywhere, inlaid on the furniture and embroidered on the silk hangings and cushions, and on the netting of the casement curtains.[29]

Miraculously, this apartment exists today and has been open to the public as the Musée Clemenceau since 1931, for after Montesquiou moved out in 1894, the apartment was taken over by Georges Clemenceau (1841–1929), who at the time was editor of the journal *L'Aurore*. He lived there until his death. Then a group of admirers put up the funds to preserve the abode of this statesman popularly known as "the Tiger." While Clemenceau's furnishings are far different from Montesquiou's, the ambiance of the silent, airless apartment and its small garden looking directly toward the Eiffel Tower has remained hauntingly unchanged since the day Robert finally found solitude there (fig. 32).

Not total solitude, however, for in 1885 Montesquiou had encountered the individual who would become his intimate companion until this friend's death twenty years later. Gabriel Yturri (fig. 34), the man in question, was born at Tucumán in northern Argentina on March 12, 1864 (a Piscean like Montesquiou). In his teens Yturri had been taken away from the civil unrest in his country by an English clergyman working with the Red Cross, the Rev. Kenelm Vaughan, and placed in a school in Lisbon run by English Dominican friars. Somehow the young man made it to Paris, where he was introduced to Robert de Montesquiou on Monday, March 16, 1885. Their meeting took place in the galleries of the École des Beaux-Arts, setting for the vast Delacroix exhibition that had opened ten days earlier. Montesquiou recalled that "this young Argentinian, only recently arrived in the capital, had heard talk of me here, in a manner that had seduced him." [30] The reaction must have been mutual, for soon this "young savage, the Chactas of Chateaubriand"— referring to the hero of Chateaubriand's novel *Atala* [31]—was ensconced in an apartment near Robert's and engaged as his secretary.

Just turned twenty-one, Yturri had, in his mentor's thirty-year-old eyes, "the features of a young hero of antiquity, proud, able-bodied, and graceful, [with] eyes the color of a roasted coffee bean." [32] In addition to his physical attributes, the young man was bright, passionately interested in the arts, and abubble with enthusiasm about everything. He was also by nature prone to serve, as suggested by this note he addressed Robert

36 Studio Fotografico, Bordighera, *Portrait of Montesquiou and Yturri,* photocard, 1888, Glasgow University Library

early on in their relationship: "You know that I am devoted to you, body and soul, and for all my life. So use me as you wish. I would give everything to spare you any moments of sadness." [33] Yturri did indeed serve his master in myriad ways, practical as well as emotional, often saying to him, "I came to humanize you." [34]

In order to impose Yturri on his august circle of acquaintances, Montesquiou simply ennobled him as Don Gabriel de Yturri, citing the distinguished lineage of the latter's mother Genoveva Surita. While some, most especially Robert's father, resisted, most people gave in to Yturri's charm, his perfect manners, and the fact that they couldn't have Robert's company without his friend's. The poet flaunted their affection in the face of conservative reaction, as in these lines dedicating the 1906 edition of *Les Hortensias bleus* to Yturri the year after his death:

> *Un honneur me viendra d'avoir aimé sans feinte,*
> *Ce qui n'inspire encore à d'autres, que la crainte* [35]

Whistler surely encountered Yturri in Robert's company, both in London, where the two were ensconced during early work on the poet's portrait in 1891, and subsequently in Paris. But the artist never mentioned him in any of his letters to Montesquiou nor, surprisingly, in any to his wife, Beatrice. She, however, seems to have been less rigid and referred to Yturri with familiarity and understanding in this note she sent Montesquiou in the spring of 1892:

> This is most kind of you, and it is very funny—that the Knight of the flowers should appear again on the scene. We shall be very glad of his services, but it will be later on, when the time comes for the furniture, and all that belongs to the ornamental part, which would be natural to him. [36]

Beatrice also revealed here the significance of the title of Montesquiou's memorial to Yturri—*Le Chancelier de fleurs*—as referring to his frequent appearance as the bearer of bouquets sent by the poet.

Robert later regretted that he had never commissioned a major portrait of his companion, though he was pleased with the pastel Louise Breslau executed after him, which Montesquiou bequeathed to the Musée Lambinet at Versailles, and with La Gandara's chalk drawing of Yturri reading (fig. 35). The caricaturist Sem (Goursat, called Sem, 1863–1943), frequently depicted Yturri at Robert's side, exaggerating his nubbly hair and the mole on his chin from which a single hair curled up (fig. 37). When travelling, the two men were frequently photographed, as in an early portrait taken at Bordighera (fig. 36).

Most of those who bothered to recall Yturri did so with sympathy. The caricaturist Ferdinand Bac (1859–1952), who wrote savagely about Montesquiou, had this to say of his friend:

> He was, it seems, a salesman in the men's glove department in a store near the Madeleine.…He had velvet eyes, a particular genius for a servitude that he fully accepted, an adoration for the lord of the Hydrangeas, a devotion, a taste for the arts and antiquities. And what else? [37]

The Duchesse de Clermont-Tonnerre analyzed the relations of Montesquiou and Yturri with deep understanding, writing of this man with his "cooing and guttural accent":

> Montesquiou represented for him the whole historic past of France, all the painters, all the books, all the charms, and all the

40

37 Sem, *Montesquiou and Yturri in Evening Clothes,* colored lithograph, n.d., New York, Frick Collection

seductions of the intellect. The child of the sun [Yturri] knew henceforth before what altar he should kneel, and from that day [of their meeting] forth, his ardor, his ingenuity, and his enthusiasm were cast at the feet of the celebrated count. To realize his desires was to collaborate in the creation of a work of beauty and of the unexpected. I never saw a believer so enthusiastic as Gabriel. He literally wore himself out, not only in serving better, but even more in enlarging the divinity of his god....So long as Yturri lived, Montesquiou could believe in his star, situated at the highest point of the zenith.[38]

Finally, Léon Daudet, who despised Montesquiou, had this to say of his slave:

Gabriel de Yturri in my opinion was far superior in intelligence and sensitivity to his super-pretentious master....Yes, but behind [Yturri's] verbal farts, which were the delight of all around, there was watching an eye that was clear, observant, and cold. This unusual young man has remained for me a living enigma....He seemed detached from everything, though apparently attached to a thousand trifles. He had a warm heart, frenetic gestures, a sense of poetic enthusiasm, and he saw almost everything in black, as a flame held over the great abyss of nothingness.[39]

While Yturri's attentions may have preoccupied Montesquiou in private, where alone the young man was permitted to address him as "Robert" rather than as "Monsieur le Comte," there were a number of women who also played important roles in the poet's life. Among the earliest, appropriately, was the actress Sarah Bernhardt (1844–1923), whom Robert recalled meeting in the mid 1870s. It even seems likely that the two had some sort of sexual union, however brief, as Montesquiou hinted delicately in his memoirs: "When I knew her [I] had the honor, I believe I can affirm it, of inspiring in her a very real sympathy, of which she then showed me the most genuine signs." [40] If so, it must have been a unique experience for Robert. In the future he focused on women whom he could admire, refine, and display as living works of art.

A most revealing example along the way was the Comtesse Verasis de Castiglione, née Virginia Oldoini (1837–99), a woman Montesquiou never saw until moments before the lid of her coffin was lowered. This extraordinary figure had first come to Paris from her native Italy in 1855, sent by the statesman Count Cavour to obtain Napoleon III's support in the approaching war between Piedmont and Austria. Though Montesquiou believed her relations with the Emperor were of the purest, most of the countess' contemporaries and subsequent historians believed she was his mistress, and as such exerted considerable political power at the imperial court. After Napoleon's fall in 1870, the beautiful Comtesse de Castiglione withdrew into near total seclusion, like Garbo, and remained like her twentieth-century counterpart a subject of intense interest until her death nearly thirty years later.

What attracted Montesquiou to this figure was her inaccessibility, coupled with the fame she had achieved by the multiplication of her image through photography (fig. 38). Over the years, Pierre-Louis Pierson and Léopold-Ernest Mayer took some seven hundred different images of the countess, from her triumphant years at the court of the Tuileries until the end, when she was fat, toothless, and bald. Eventually Montesquiou came to own 433 of these photographs, all now preserved at The Metropolitan Museum of Art.[41] What makes them so special is that the countess staged each one herself, selecting the pose, clothing, lighting, and the peculiar dramatic suggestion that each possessed. The photographers had little to do beyond pressing their shutters, making the prints, and hand-coloring them as the subject dictated.

To return to the countess' coffin, Montesquiou somehow managed to join the intimate group of her friends gathered around it. In the extraordinary volume he published in 1913, *La Divine Comtesse, Étude d'après Madame de Castiglione,* the poet recorded his impressions of what he saw:

> A countenance of a sculptural quality, with imposing proportions, bold lines, and rigid planes, in which the brow, magnificent and broad, attracted my eye and held it, as a focus of light. The banal expression *it was like a flash of lightning* takes on here a real significance, grandeur, and precision; [for] there was for me a flash in the pale and sudden apparition of this beautiful, this grave, this noble face of death, about to disappear forever. But these epithets are insufficient; there was still more, in these features, of the *august* and the *heroic.* Yes, what struck me, in this cast of features, during this rapid minute and the memory that it left me of them, was that it seemed less supernatural than superhuman, almost without sex; that one could just as well have taken it to be that of a great man, an illustrious captain, or a famous poet. Is that not appropriate? Was she not of a virile spirit, being both *domination* and *poetry?*[42]

If Montesquiou's obsessive preoccupation with the Comtesse de Castiglione represented one extreme of his relations with the opposite sex, his near-lifelong involvement with the Comtesse Greffulhe was evidence of another, more human, and reciprocal kind. The Princesse Élisabeth de Caraman-Chimay (1860–1952) was his cousin, his grandparents Anatole and Élodie being her great-grandparents. Five years younger than Robert, Élisabeth confided to her diary at the age of seventeen that he "ought to make a charming husband" for her.[43] Instead their relationship became one of mentor and pupil. Montesquiou introduced his beautiful cousin to artists and men of letters, shared her musical enthusiasms as well as her interest in the occult, advised her on her wardrobe (including a black velvet gown with bat-wing sleeves), and was more likely to be her companion in society than the formidable and colossally rich Comte Henry Greffulhe she had married at the age of eighteen. As Comtesse Greffulhe she was reigning queen of Parisian society for more than half a century, actively involved in the artistic, scientific, and political life of the capital. Her awesome appearance led Proust to consider her the most beautiful woman in Europe and to implore her, in vain, for a photograph of herself (fig. 39).

Her cousin sang her praises far and wide, in poetry and in prose, perhaps most evocatively with the text he devoted to her in *La Divine Comtesse:*

> In the years following her marriage, when she [Comtesse Greffulhe] assumed the position of the conquering beauty, her movement through a salon added rapidity to intensity. She would

38 P.-L. Pierson and L.-E. Mayer,
*Comtesse Castiglione Holding a Frame as
Mask,* albumen photoprint, n.d., New
York, Metropolitan Museum of Art,
provenance Montesquiou

39 P. Nadar, *Portrait of Comtesse
Greffulhe*, albumen photoprint, n.d.,
Paris, private collection, frame designed
by Montesquiou

40 P. Helleu, *Comtesse Greffulhe Playing
Billiards,* watercolor, 1891, France,
private collection

41 C. Popelin, *Portrait of Robert de
Montesquiou,* enamel, 1891, Paris, Galerie
Elstir, provenance Princesse Mathilde

arrive with the elegant speed, and at the same time the delicate
majesty, of a gazelle, that might have picked up a piece of black
velvet that it dragged after itself with infinite grace. Always
accompanied by an ambassador, some celebrated old man, a
famous artist, or an illustrious scientist, she would advance
through the wake and swirl of the tide whose paradoxical nature
was to eclipse all the rest with the darkness of her train.
But her eyes were more velvety than her gown; the hair, in those
times dressed high, rose as in a vapor, like the incense of an
agreeable sacrifice, and her clear laughter, occasionally a little
nervous or dry, marked her pleasure in pleasing and the
determination to excel at it. She fulfilled this promise always.[44]
In response to such adulation, the Comtesse Greffulhe had this
to say:

> I don't think there is in this world a pleasure comparable to that
> of the woman who feels herself, in this way, the object of all eyes,
> from which she derives joy and energy. A feeling composed of a
> surfeit of life and happiness, of pride, intoxication, generosity,
> domination, of royalty proffered and rejected. Only great poets,
> great captains, great orators must experience these sensations, on
> that day when their bravery and their talent make them acclaim-
> ed in brilliant demonstrations.[45]

And once when Montesquiou quoted his favorite line about his
cousin to her and her sister— *"Beau lis qui regardez avec vos pistils noirs"*—
Élisabeth said, "Very like me, isn't it, Ghislaine?" [46]

Robert could always rely on the Comtesse Greffulhe to give his
receptions their final touch of brilliance, though she invariably appeared
late and remained so brief a time that her appearances were in the nature
of apparitions. He called on her to charm Whistler when the time came,
and he regretted that she did not have her beauty immortalized by the
artist. She rather preferred Helleu, who left some memorable images of
the countess, captured in moments of intimacy and fun (fig. 40). Even
when Montesquiou was once on the verge of breaking off their friendship
over some imagined infraction of his rules, she warned him that it
would be useless to try. Until his final days, the Comtesse Greffulhe was
providing him with practical and emotional assistance, finally teaching
him how to die. In 1920 the poet became the godfather of the countess'
granddaughter Corisande de Gramont, who would eventually inherit
much of his precious memorabilia.

In 1894 Montesquiou left his apartment in the rue Franklin and
moved with Yturri to a residence in the town of Versailles, at 93 avenue de
Paris (fig. 72). This "Pavillon Montesquiou" would be the setting for a
number of the poet's "rather magnificent" receptions (fig. 43).[47] Yet to
Edmond de Goncourt, Montesquiou spoke of the simple joys of life away
from Paris, as the older writer noted in his journal: "Then he goes on
about the happiness of his life in the pavilion where he has set himself up
in Versailles, about the separation that occurs between the gentleman
in his blue smock of that place and the gentleman dressed up for Paris,
about the satisfaction of not being subject to an unexpected visit." [48]
It was here that Montesquiou finally took possession of his portrait by
Whistler after its appearance at the Salon of 1894. Unfortunately, none of

the photographs of the pavilion or descriptions of its interiors indicate where it hung.

The isolation from Paris proved less appealing after two years. Montesquiou and Yturri returned there in 1896, the poet setting himself up in a third-floor apartment in the hôtel at 80 rue de l'Université that had belonged to his mother and now belonged to him. Yturri took an apartment nearby. Two years later, in Yturri's absence, Montesquiou moved into a ground-floor apartment at 14 avenue Bosquet, where he lived until 1900.

It was during this period, in 1897, that Giovanni Boldini (1842–1931) executed his celebrated portrait of Montesquiou (fig. 95), so totally different from Whistler's. In his memoirs, curiously enough, the poet does not speak of this work, its commission, genesis, or meaning for himself. Some critics who viewed it at the Salon of the Champ de Mars in 1897 were put off by the painting's mannered perfection. One noted: "The Comte Robert de Montesquiou is certainly, along with M. Coquelin the younger and Mlle Yvette Guilbert, the personality the most portrayed of modern Paris.…We see him again this spring, executed by Boldini, the habitual deformer of little, agitated, and grimacing ladies, otherwise known as the Paganini of the *peignoirs*." [49] The critic of *Le Rappel* failed even to see Montesquiou in the portrait:

> Visitors to the latest Salon were able to see, signed by Boldini, the truly admirable portrait of a cane, with a knob of turquoise or lapis-lazuli [*sic*]. This cane obtained a brilliant success. Very well enhanced by its placement, of a perfect resemblance, the gold of the rim and the reflections of the stone dazzling, it is a delight for the eye.…In short, a little masterpiece of a still life. [50]

But the general reaction to this sober and structured masterpiece was enthusiastic, and the subject wrote with delight to his painter: "A character of Shelley's, the Magus Zoroaster, encountered himself one day while walking in his garden. The same thing just happened to me, in a much nicer way, since the second me encountered by the first was signed by you.…The gratitude of the model is linked with his great admiration for the painter, with his deep attachment to the friend." [51]

The famous cane in this portrait would involve Montesquiou in his first duel. Following the disastrous fire that took place at the Bazar de la Charité on May 4, 1897, claiming 140 high-society victims, rumors circulated that certain gentlemen present at this fund-raising event had saved themselves by striking at women in their path with their canes. Soon thereafter Montesquiou found himself with some friends visiting the collection of the Baronne Adolphe de Rothschild, who had invited as well the poet Henri de Régnier, his wife, and two sisters-in-law. On extremely fragile terms with Montesquiou, one of the latter, as Montesquiou recalled, "seeing a beautiful cane I was holding in my hand, observed, with a frankly hostile tone, that it was of a size to clear a way for oneself in a catastrophe." [52] Montesquiou, who had been at home at the time of the disaster, demanded satisfaction for this insult from Régnier and fought him soon thereafter. Hopelessly unskilled with a sword, the former was lightly wounded, but he did save his reputation.

Montesquiou's next residence, at 96 avenue Maillot in the suburb of Neuilly, facing the Bois de Boulogne, was another discovery of Yturri's.

42 A. Besnard, *Montesquiou in the Allée Royale at Versailles,* (frontispiece for *Les Perles rouges*), etching, 1899, Paris, private collection

The poet said the latter appeared before him one day like a figure in a tapestry bearing a tiny palace on a platter. Soon named the "Pavillon des Muses," this was to be their most celebrated abode. The house was large and, though of fairly recent construction, had a convincing Louis XVI air outside and a genuine set of Louis XV panelling in the major salon.

The many receptions that occurred here were characterized by their host as being no longer merely "magnificent," but "superb." [53] These events were elaborately orchestrated by Montesquiou and really constituted works of art, in the modern sense of "happenings." Utilizing his own collections and free to borrow from the stock of the great dealer in the decorative arts Georges Hoentschel, the poet evoked in his memoirs what he achieved:

> He [Hoentschel] opened up for me his workshops, putting at my disposal wall hangings, tapestries, rugs; I utilized all that in a state of drunken delirium, and when the freshly cut roses had scattered themselves along the stretches of Savonnerie, when the invisible music brought life to the upper terraces or the hidden musicians' balconies, when the rare fruits and the dainty titbits, revived from ancient recipes, vied with the colors of the old ceramic dishes, finally, when I saw moving about, in the midst of these elements of heightened sensitivity and abundance, women in the latest fashions challenging one another with their successful inventions, I experienced a ravishing pleasure. [54]

As to whether or not he was a good host, Montesquiou had this to say: "I sometimes asked myself that; no doubt I was, a little despotically. That is, I liked my receptions better than I liked my guests, who perhaps perceived this. I always considered them a complementary detail inseparable from—should I say inevitable to?—a reception, but as a detail, alas! too often recalcitrant." [55]

Once again, Montesquiou opened his house to the press, whose articles and photographs constitute a valuable record of the interiors and particularly of the placement of major works of art. Thus we learn that Whistler's portrait of the poet stood in the dining room next to the majestic fireplace (fig. 73), Boldini's was placed on an easel in the White Salon to the right of the door leading into the Salon of the Roses, a drawing by Ingres of Liszt (untraceable) sat on the piano in the Music Room, Helleu drypoints decorated the boudoir, and the bedroom contained the now-familiar collection of bats, described by their owner thus: "...a whole case is filled with the collection of these singular birds, in lacquer, ivory, bronze, porcelain, and rock crystal, all worked to show the bizarre contours of these winged mammals full of mystery and dreams." [56]

Perhaps Montesquiou's most original creation, and one which, like Whistler's "breakfasts," would have a revival in our day, was the utilization of perfume in his interiors. This phenomenon was described by an unknown journalist in *La Liberté:*

> Finally, he has the fantasy, which can be qualified as genial, of introducing, for the very first time, *perfume* into the art of decorating. The visitor who crosses the threshold of his *home* has his olfactory nerve titillated by subtle odors, each one having a symbolic meaning. A perfume burner was placed in the room where one eats; another, in the room where one smokes; another,

in the bedroom; another in the room where one chats. And I really believe that, according to the nature of the conversation, the scents differ, and that the one which encourages flirtation is not the one that encourages political discussion.[57]

Once, in August 1901, thieves broke into the Pavillon des Muses while Montesquiou was away in the Pyrenees. Rushing back to survey the damage, the poet's greatest fear was that some "inestimable work of art such as my portrait by Whistler [might have been] lacerated by disappointed and frenzied brutes." But, to his great surprise and delight, nothing had been removed but some of his perfume burners. When apprehended, the thieves declared that they hadn't taken anything else because "there was nothing there for us," a judgment the poet savored.[58] It is ironic that at this moment Montesquiou should have described the value of his portrait by Whistler as being "inestimable." At some point in 1901 he did decline an offer of 50,000 francs for it, but in October of 1902 he would sell it for 60,000 (see pp. 97–98).

The following January, Montesquiou, Yturri, and their steel-grey Great Dane, the latter sporting an "ivory-white leather collar set with large turquoises,"[59] set sail for New York. The purpose for the trip was a series of seven lectures that the theatrical impresario Elizabeth Marbury, via Yturri, had contracted with Montesquiou for the rumored sum of 175,000 francs. Marbury was well aware of the poet's constant need of financial refueling, as she noted in her memoirs: "Montesquiou's poverty was a proverbially acute condition with him, and had it not been for his devoted henchman, Gabriel D'Yturri, I fear that he would have been frequently overtaken by dire distress."[60]

On subjects as diverse as "Versailles," "Mystery," and "Travel," the lectures were delivered by the poet in French at New York's most fashionable hotel, Sherry's, on alternating Thursdays at three o'clock. Tickets, available for the series only, cost $35. Reporters and caricaturists (figs. 46, 47) had a field day with Montesquiou, who handled them with his usual self-promotional aplomb. Always careful to list the notables—mostly women—who attended the lectures, critics were on the whole impressed by his thoughts and the manner in which he delivered them. James Montague, writing for the *New York Evening Journal,* concentrated on the poet's delivery:

> The speaker was under way again, chanting like a mediaeval monk, and his admirers were hot on his heels....It is his voice that tells the story of his emotions, as well as that of his opinions. It sobs. It wails, it exults, it deprecates, it approves, all in its changing tones and inflections. It has all the tone colors of a rainbow of sound, and is fully equal to carrying on the work of transmitting its owner's opinions of his utterances simultaneously with the utterances themselves....He is both dramatic and convincing, two qualities which very often travel quite different roads....Mrs. Astor had come early, and was among the first to tell the Comte how great a success he was.[61]

While Whistler's portrait appeared on the ten-page brochure advertising Montesquiou's lectures and was frequently referred to by reporters, some of whom even suggested the poet might have brought it along with him, it appeared in his rooms at the Westminster Hotel on

43 Unknown photographer, *The Inaugural Reception at the Pavillon Montesquiou, Versailles,* from *La Revue illustrée,* August 1, 1894, Washington, Library of Congress

La fête du 30 mai.

44 J.-L. Forain, *Portrait of Robert de Montesquiou,* oil, after 1900, Paris, private collection

Irving Place only in the guise of a photograph (fig. 66). No one seemed to know that the painting had been acquired by Richard Canfield, though at least one writer was aware that Whistler was currently at work on the latter's portrait.

If his own portrait no longer belonged to Montesquiou, what he had learned from the artist flavored more than one of the poet's lectures, as these lines from one of them attest:

> Mystery floats over his landscapes, passes through the eyes of his portraits, and alights as a velvety touch on the souls that he causes to dream and to remember....mystery in life and in art is an emanation radiating from a being or from a work of art that troubles and charms, attracts, and holds as by a promise of revelation indefinitely deferred.[62]

Back in Paris, Montesquiou fought a second duel on January 18, 1904, provoked by a insulting remark he had published about the mother of his opponent, Jean Stern. In his wild manipulation of the sword— he was described in the press as "ignorant of all or almost all of the art of arms"[63]—the poet accidentally wounded Stern's doctor before he himself was sufficiently injured for the duel to be halted. Among the many notes Montesquiou received afterwards was a characteristic telegram from the writer Jean Lorrain saying, "I am with you wholeheartedly against *the Jew*."[64]

On July 6, 1905, Yturri expired after a long battle with diabetes. To the astonishment of many, Montesquiou arranged that his friend be buried in the Cimetière des Gonards at Versailles in a tomb that was intended to receive the poet as well one day. The unmarked grave is surmounted by a large lead figure of a winged angel or Eros with a finger to his lips, which the two friends named "The Angel of Silence" (fig. 51). Yturri had discovered this work years before at the château of Vitry and had wanted to buy it, but in fact Montesquiou acquired it only after Yturri's death. It had by then found a home in England and had to be recovered. Yturri and Montesquiou admired the unusual and slightly ambiguous connotation of the statue's gesture, as well as the more traditional symbolism of the elements at the base: a dog (fidelity) and a vanquished serpent (envy). While Montesquiou and Yturri believed the work to date from the seventeenth century, the sculpture specialist James Draper feels that it more likely dates from the early nineteenth century and might have been modelled by a neoclassical artist such as Augustin-Félix Fortin (1763–1832), who exhibited at the Salon of 1819 a *Harpocrates, God of Silence.* By coincidence, the American writer Edith Wharton would be buried near Yturri and Montesquiou in 1937.

Montesquiou next set about creating a proper literary memorial for Yturri. Seeking information on his friend's early years from the English clergyman who had first brought Gabriel to Europe, he wrote him that "life goes on for me, desolate, isolated, and blurred by the loss of the companion who filled it to overflowing, for twenty years, with his affectionate and effective enthusiasm."[65] The result was an extraordinary book, *Le Chancelier de fleurs,* which Montesquiou had privately printed in an edition of one hundred in 1907. In it he compared his sorrow with that of Edmond de Goncourt mourning his beloved brother Jules, or with that of Montaigne regretting the loss of his friend La Boétie, of whom the

45 Montesquiou, *Self-Portrait,* pen and ink, c. 1897(?), Paris, Bibliothèque Nationale de France, Département des Manuscrits

essayist wrote: "We shared everything by halves; now I feel I am robbing him of his part." [66] Erasing any suggestion of carnality from this record of his relationship with Yturri, Montesquiou described it as the most elevated example of pure friendship, something beyond the comprehension of most mortals. Then, as if for a mass in one year's mind, the poet invited some forty friends to a memorial reception at which he read from *Le Chancelier de fleurs.* Those who had known and appreciated Yturri, such as Helleu, were moved by the event. Others, such as Ferdinand Bac, were suspicious of Montesquiou's motives, seeing this as an occasion for the poet to be sublime in the elegiac mode or simply to offend the conservative attitudes of his family.

By 1909 the poet could no longer continue to rent the Pavillon des Muses, nor could he afford to purchase it, so once again he moved— this time to a farther suburb of Paris near Saint-Germain-en-Laye, called Le Vésinet, where he established himself in an imitation of the Grand Trianon he called the "Palais Rose." This, Montesquiou's final abode, had been the discovery of his new secretary, Henri Pinard.

Montesquiou amply merited the appellation "poet and writer." His bibliography includes over eighty items (many of which appeared in multiple editions and in translations), comprising volumes of poetry, novels, essays, critical articles, texts of lectures, prefaces, and memoirs. His correspondence, of which a good part has been preserved, was voluminous. He also was meticulous about preserving correspondence he received, as evident in the 369 thick volumes of the "Papiers de Robert de Montesquiou" preserved in the Département des Manuscrits at the Bibliothèque Nationale de France. Appropriate to the emblems he had chosen for himself, among his first publications were the volumes of poetry *Les Chauves-Souris* (1892) and *Les Hortensias bleus* (1896). The three volumes of this acerbic gentleman's memoirs, *Les Pas effacés,* were anticipated by his contemporaries with some apprehension. When published posthumously in 1923, they were considered rather tame.

Much as he sought praise for his literary efforts, Montesquiou never established the reputation he dreamed of. For example, when he was living at Versailles, a hesitant Yturri appeared before him one day with the latest *Le Figaro,* containing an article by the art critic Arsène Alexandre entitled "Opinions, Études de moeurs" that read in part as follows:

> Monsieur Jacques Saint-Cère wittily calls Monsieur de Montesquiou a "sculptor of clouds." I should rather prefer to name him a stringer of pearls [i.e., a trifler]. In days of yore… grand aristocrats used to purchase beautiful furniture and protect beautiful poets without feeling themselves obliged to rhyme and pick up the compass.…Even in our day, he [the aristocrat] had enough flair to surround himself with gifted poets and distinguished artists instead of thinking of becoming their rival, to have his attempts at art judged by sculptors and painters and to honor his poetry with a preface signed by Leconte de Lisle [referring to *Les Chauves-Souris*]. His intentions were good, though a little frail, but they have gone astray. [67]

In reply, Montesquiou cited a number of writers burdened like himself with a title and a nobiliary particle who still had managed to rise above the condition of the mere "amateur." Alexandre apparently gave in, for around 1905 he offered Montesquiou his gold-point portrait by Alphonse Legros to supplement a group of literary portraits that the poet had assembled.

Harsher and more in tune with the majority of Montesquiou's critics was the opinion of Paul Morand, who wrote:

> Montesquiou has polished a thousand sonnets with a hand jewelled with black pearls and will leave behind nothing but a few modern-style curiosities and some imitations of Mallarmé written in red ink and sprinkled with gold dust. A personality of the most curious, because entirely phony, from a period of dazzling falsifiers and of pious or impious lies. He will survive thanks only to the des Esseintes of Huysmans and the Baron de Charlus of Proust. Montesquiou was right to frequent men of letters.[68]

Montesquiou delighted in the spoken word as well as the printed one, and could go on indefinitely, whether from the podium, in society, or with an auditor in his home. It is little known that one of Montesquiou's most appreciative listeners was the art historian and dealer Bernard Berenson (1865–1959), who often saw him during the summer at Saint-Moritz. In 1904, Berenson wrote to Isabella Stewart Gardner: "Most of all have I enjoyed Montesquiou. The other day I was alone with him nine hours. He talked steadily, and not a moment was dull. Most of it had the brilliance of a genius." [69] Some twenty years later, Berenson took pains to explain to the future American print connoisseur A. Hyatt Mayor (1901–80) just how he thought the verbiage of Montesquiou came to be used by Proust in the creation of *A la recherche du temps perdu*. This gloss on such an important subject became available only recently with the publication of a selection of Mayor's notes, which includes the following:

> But all Marcel Proust's minute [descriptions] of the sentiments he had gotten, like his second-hand knowledge of the "monde," from Comte Robert de Montesquiou.…[Montesquiou] had a horror of being alone and as strong a love for his own voice, so he would talk 20 hours a day to anyone who would listen, verbal portraits in all Marcel Proust's length and delicacy of all the "monde," of his servants; and his coterie would sit about and, to keep him at it, adjust a button if missing. Between this profound analysis he would make Jesuitically neat essays on ethics. He was a great genius of talk, but could not write it. B.B. [Berenson] said that next to Proust he had heard more than anybody else.…Thus B.B. knew well the materials for the work [*A la recherche*], for de M. is not M. de Charlus…but all the book. De M. was the last and greatest of the bards and Marcel Proust had the power de M. lacked to give the oft-told tale a form and project it three dimensionally.…The material of the work is too vast to be one man's work. It took all de M.'s genius to gather it, all Proust's to shape it.…As de M. would talk to anyone who listened intelligently and as long as they had strength for it, and as Proust had all day empty to haul it in, he got more than anybody else.[70]

Anyone who has written seriously on Proust has had to consider the significance of his relations with Montesquiou, whom he called his "professor of beauty," and the extent to which the younger writer drew

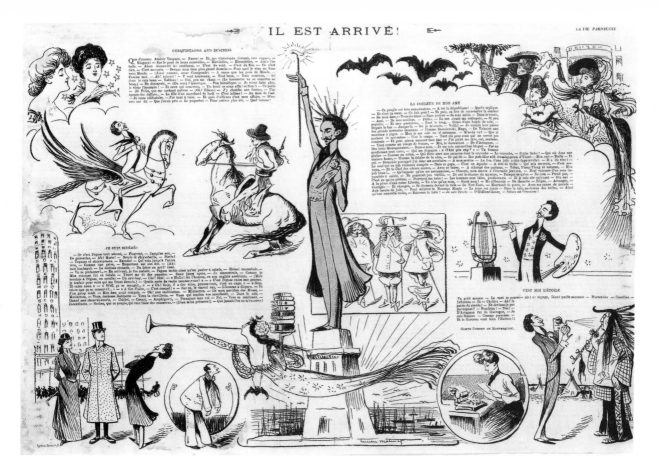

46 L. Métivet, *Il est arrivé!,* from
La Vie parisienne, February 14, 1903,
Washington, Library of Congress

from this experience to create the character of the Baron de Charlus.
As Robert Proust recalled in his introduction to the 1930 edition of his
brother's letters to Montesquiou, the two had first met at a reception
given by the artist Madeleine Lemaire in 1893, and their friendship
continued until Montesquiou's death twenty-eight years later. Its ardor
diminished as Proust's reputation grew, first with the publication of
Du côté de chez Swann in 1913, then when he won the Prix Goncourt in
1919. But earlier on, Montesquiou had drawn the young man's features,
probably from a photograph (fig. 93). The younger man had also given
the poet a *carnet de bal* with a mother-of-pearl cover, which Montesquiou
in turn gave to Madame Helleu (fig. 48). But as each successive volume
of Proust's opus was published, Montesquiou was confronted again
and again with the fascinating but unsavory character of the Baron de
Charlus, who seemed more and more to resemble himself in his
appearance, his behavior, and his conversation. The poet well knew he
was not alone in seeing these parallels. Finally, when Montesquiou, in the
year of his death, pointedly questioned Proust about his inspiration for
Charlus, Proust evasively cited the late Baron Doazan as one source, but
stressed that he had made the character into someone "much more vast,
entirely invented…my character was created before I began to write…
and I think he is much larger, contains much more of a diverse humanity
than if I had limited him to his resemblance with Monsieur D[oazan]….
Besides…I extract a generality from out of a thousand unconscious
reminiscences." [71]

47 Vet, *As Comte de Montesquiou seemed to "Vet,"* from *New York Herald,* February 6, 1903, New York Public Library

Regarding this as so much obfuscation, Montesquiou took revenge, rather childishly, in his memoirs. There he wrote of "our young man":

> He is the author of an abstruse book, inextricable, for which he has, to start with, found a lovely title….It is, to begin with, a sort of autobiography, where there are some pretty things, interlaced with horrors, as if for fun, a slightly sadistic fun, since the first are family memories, and, the second, scenes of lesbianism, the whole finishing by turning into pandemonium, through a lack of editing, of taste, and of selection….He is always sick, or at least in bed, surrounded with respiratory machines to ward off his asthmatic crises; there are also pots of preserves and chamber pots.[72]

Montesquiou became something of a recluse during his final years, though he could still succeed at establishing new friendships with figures such as Gabriele D'Annunzio and the dancer Ida Rubinstein, whose androgynous beauty fascinated him (fig. 49). With the coming of World War I, he fled the Palais Rose and retreated to the Château d'Artagnan. There, in his solitude he composed some of his most serious poetry, published in 1915 as *Les Offrandes blessées, élégies guerrières*. But once back at Le Vésinet after the war, he realized that, at an hour's distance from Paris, it was too far to attract frequent visitors. Even worse, Montesquiou perceived that the world he had once dominated no longer existed, that his fortune was gone, and his vaunted beauty as well. To a young man who had caught his fancy, the aging poet wrote: "I very much liked to be seen, but I don't like it anymore at all. One loves only what one does well, and to display oneself is not for every age." [73]

One can only admire the frankness with which Montesquiou then contemplated his situation and the clarity with which he described it in his memoirs:

> A strange sensation, more strange than painful, is that of perceiving all of a sudden, brusquely, without warning, almost without having seen it coming, *that one's life is over.* There one is, more or less worn out physically, or still strong, one's faculties apparently intact, but ill-adjusted to the taste of the day; one feels disaffected, a stranger to contemporary civilization which one had occasionally anticipated, but whose present manifestations hurt and shock less than they seem vain. In a word, a watertight bulkhead separates you from the artistic conceptions of Picasso, of the Czechoslovakian esthetic, or African art, and that is not a good way to feel up-to-date.[74]

By November 1920 Montesquiou realized that he was suffering from uremia, a blood infection, and began treatments for it that involved stays in clinics. From there he would complain sorrowfully about the food to the Comtesse Greffulhe, who urged him, in response, to understand why the "English call a sick person *the patient*…what an appropriate term!" [75] In the spring of 1921 she urged him to consider taking two steps to resolve his dilemmas: "…sell some knick-knacks in order to restore your health" and, more surprisingly, "get married!!!!! Providence must make us encounter a widow of a certain age—very rich—who would see in you the one who would bring her *the glory of bearing his name.*" [76]

48 French, *Dance-Card Case*, leather and mother-of-pearl, 1890s, Paris, private collection, provenance Proust and Montesquiou

As this came to naught, the Comtesse Greffulhe tried to assist her cousin by offering him the services of her staff, the use of her Panhard, and other practical attentions. Then, finally grasping the hopelessness of his situation, she wrote him this remarkable letter:

Thus, with tranquility of soul, of mind, and of body, you will reach the plateau of serenity so necessary to attain in order to "produce yet another fruit," not only one, but many—fruits of your maturity—while waiting for old age—which people so often vilify and which is, to my mind, the most beautiful period in the life of a vigorous soul in all the possession of its thought, of its memories, the order by which they are arranged, and for the joy of feeling oneself delivered of the encumbrance, one can thus prepare oneself, slowly, gently, for the thought of the *transfiguration* of our chrysalis—without bitterness and then fall in a natural way from the earthly tree as the ripe fruit whose supreme delight consists in being savored by a God.[77]

Montesquiou addressed a few notes to friends informing them of his condition and must have read with morbid interest responses such as this one from the theatrical designer Léon Bakst: "Your letter moved me. I felt a single, heavy tear course down my cheek—not that my nerves have remained too tender—but the fragility of human life, which is at the same time its beauty, is conveyed so vividly by the voice of a friend, by your profound and submissive thought." [78]

Montesquiou left the Palais Rose in November 1921, with the stated intention of spending the winter months at Menton, but probably with the expectation of dying there. He and Pinard settled into the Hôtel des Îles Britanniques, whence the secretary set out for Orléans to pick up the first copies of Montesquiou's latest book, *Élus et appelés.*

The author intended to send the first copy to Ida Rubinstein, but he never completed the letter to accompany it, which he had begun on December 3 or 4. Pinard piously preserved this document, which reads:

You are going to find [enclosed] the *first copy* of my *thirteenth volume* of essays (*Élus et appelés*) which I happily succeeded [in having produced] *according to my wishes,* and which will remain in your life as the passing through of a man who is suffering and who is threatened with being unable to bring to a successful conclusion the *manifestations of his art* and the justifications of his impartiality. That alone troubles me and I am not good at enduring the excruciating pain it causes me.[79]

The next document concerning Montesquiou is his death certificate. Thereon, Maurice Butot, undertaker, and Jean-Baptiste Calvy, civil administrator, attested that "Marie Joseph Robert Anatole Comte de Montesquiou Fezensac, unmarried man of letters," had died in his hotel room at two o'clock Sunday morning on December 11, 1921.[80] He was sixty-six years old.

Pinard arranged that the body be transported to Versailles, where a funeral mass was scheduled for noon on December 21 in the modest church of Sainte-Élisabeth, near the Cimetière des Gonards where the poet was to be buried alongside Yturri.

Disturbed by this detail and unmentioned in the will (Pinard was the principal heir), the Montesquiou family decided to schedule a mass

55

49 Unknown photographer, *Ida Rubinstein in "Le Martyre de Saint-Sébastien,"* albumen photoprint, 1911, New York, Paul F. Walter, frame designed by Montesquiou

50 P. A. de László, *Portrait of Robert de Montesquiou,* oil, 1905, Paris, private collection

for the repose of the soul of their uncle, granduncle, and cousin two days earlier at the church of Saint-Pierre de Chaillot in Paris. There was a large turnout of notables at this event, including two of Montesquiou's favorites, Forain and Helleu.

The funeral mass was a different affair. Planned entirely by Montesquiou as his final "reception," its character was described as one of "grandiose simplicity."[81] The coffin, which had first been set up in a mortuary chapel illuminated with tapers, was moved to a catafalque, surrounded with more candles, in the chancel. In the manner of ancient royal funerals, the interior of the church was hung with black draperies embroidered with silver stars. Canon Froissard from the Cathedral of Versailles celebrated the mass; the absolution was given by Father Cayre, pastor of Sainte-Élisabeth. In no particular order, *Le Figaro* noted the following among the mourners: "Mme Ida Rubinstein, M. and Mme Helleu, M. and Mme Émile Straus, M. Maurice Barrès, Duchesse de Clermont-Tonnerre, Comtesse de Noailles, Comtesse de Sommyèvre, Comte and Comtesse de Boisrouvray, Lady Michelham, Comte de Gabriac, M. André Maurel, Monsieur de Montferrat, Professeur Albert Robin, M. and Mme Lobre, M. Fischoff, Miss Natalie Barney."[82] The Comtesse Greffulhe was not mentioned.

At the graveside, Docteur Paul-Louis Couchoud, disciple of the mystic writer Ernest Hello (1828–85) and a friend of Montesquiou, delivered an oration that deserves to be quoted here, at least in part:

He [Montesquiou] chose the little church where he wanted to stop for an hour...and here he is, arrived at the end of his earthly voyage, at the beautiful resting place where he interred, some fifteen years ago, his very dear friend and where he has come to occupy, alongside him, the place he had reserved for himself.... Today let us weep for the poet who knew how to weep nobly. We shall see no more his tall figure thrust back, his princely brow, his deep and pensive eyes, his mocking and sincere mouth. We shall hear no more the strong and gentle brassy tones of his enchanting voice. It is from this point on that his name is going to flourish. The beauty that he revealed will be more evident to his followers than to his contemporaries, who were often distracted, sometimes obtuse. Young people who are not yet born will adopt him with enthusiasm and will know more than we do, and better, what he was....At once the haughtiest and most candid of men, *proud but sensitive,* refining all proprieties and breaking all conventions, master of the art of pleasing and attracted by the *aristocratic pleasure of displeasing,* irritated to excess by the slightest baseness, infinitely exalted by the most obscure sign of spiritual grandeur, stating that *the only bearable things are things in the extreme,* longing to be loved fervently and knowing how to love with fervor, quivering at every call, the first to embrace a new form of beauty, the last to abandon the old, a firm judge of his epoch, a born poet, a legendary friend, Montesquiou promulgated a way of feeling and of living, he has assumed among French poets and among inimitable men a place that is his alone and which death, his faithful muse become his faithful servant, will know how to preserve for him.[83]

51 French, *The Angel of Silence,* lead, early nineteenth-century(?), installed as part of the Montesquiou-Yturri tomb, Cimetière des Gonards, Versailles

The poet Lucie Delarue-Mardrus (1880–1945), who read a brief poem at the cemetery, published a slightly irreverent account of the funeral in *Le Journal.* There she described "The Angel of Silence" as "standing in front of the stele, nude, a finger to his lips, a winged figure… that perhaps is an angel and no doubt is an Eros [telling us] to be quiet, and not to attempt to unravel the meaning of such a secret." She went on to reveal that three days before Montesquiou's death she had received a postcard from the poet whose message terminated with the word "Silence!" Finally, she reminded her readers:

> …the funeral ceremony, ordered by him, point by point, took place in the manner he had demanded, at once simple and stately, and nothing was lacking, not even the irony of too numerous absences, anticipated no doubt by his diabolical mischievousness.
> …So, what were they up to (the great names of his circle), three-quarters of them, the day of Montesquiou's funeral? I know some who had their names mentioned in the papers *and who were not there.*[84]

The obituaries—at least those preserved by Pinard—emphasized mostly Montesquiou's importance as an art patron and critic, such as Lucien Corpechet's in *Le Gaulois.* Its concluding paragraph provides a fitting end to the present biographical résumé:

> Open the volumes of his prose, his *Essais,* which are the collection of the articles he supplied to art journals and different Parisian magazines. You will see that all the artists of talent: painters, musicians, dancers, actors, or singers, who later on enjoyed the greatest success, the most unquestioned triumphs, were discovered, launched, or extolled by Robert de Montesquiou. All the performances that could embellish our existence, charm our eyes, enchant our ears, he pointed them out to us, he analyzed their most subtle nuances for us.[85]

The Evolution of the Portrait

A cast of characters remarkable even for the flamboyant late years of the nineteenth century participated in the drama of Whistler's painting Robert de Montesquiou, from the initial meeting of the artist and his subject in 1885 to the first public exhibition of the portrait nine years later. Two Americans were to set the project in motion: the artist John Singer Sargent and the writer Henry James (fig. 52).

By the mid 1880s, Montesquiou had become intrigued with London, probably through the influence of the Anglophile painters Paul Helleu, who once had written to him that "London is the place where one absolutely must go,"[1] and Jacques-Émile Blanche, with whom Montesquiou made his first visit to London in 1884. The following summer Montesquiou decided to return there for a week or so in June in the company of the surgeon Dr. Samuel Pozzi and the composer Prince Edmond de Polignac (fig. 93). Their common friend John Singer Sargent, then residing in Paris, wrote Henry James in London on June 29, 1885, this collective letter of introduction:

> Dear James, I remember that you once said that an occasional Frenchman was not an unpleasurable diversion to you in London, and I have been so bold as to give a card of introduction to you to two friends of mine. One is Dr S. Pozzi the man in the red gown (not always) [referring to Sargent's portrait of Pozzi wearing a red dressing gown, fig. 54], a very brilliant creature! and the other is the unique extrahuman Montesquiou of whom you may have heard Bourget speak with bitterness, but who was to Bourget [Paul Bourget, 1852–1935, French writer] to a certain extent what Whistler is to Oscar Wilde. (Take warning and do not bring them together). They are going to spend a week in London and I fancy Montesquiou will be anxious to see as much of Rossetti's and Burne-Jones' work as he can. I have given him a card to B.J., to the Comyns Carrs [Joseph William Comyns Carr (1849–1916), art critic and dramatist] and to Tadema [Sir Lawrence Alma-Tadema (1836–1912), painter of genre subjects of ancient Roman life].[2]

A letter from Edmond de Polignac to Montesquiou's cousin, then the Vicomtesse Greffulhe (fig. 39), postmarked "Calais/Paris" and dated June 27, 1885,[3] indicates that the trio had already arrived in London before Sargent sent the above letter to James, and that they were settled in the Cavendish Hotel, 81 Jermyn Street. It informed her that they were off to a performance of Handel's *Israel in Egypt* and included a newspaper clipping of a comic engraving entitled "First Attempt at An Instantaneous Photograph"—an allusion to her interest in photography as a student of Nadar.

James rose to Sargent's bait, leaving for Montesquiou at the Cavendish Hotel the following letter (in French), offering him the ultimate of attractions—Whistler:

> Dear Sir, I leave you this word in haste so that you not make any engagements for the day after tomorrow, Friday, in the evening, if possible, & that you be kind enough to put off until that time our dinner. I have just seen Whistler, who unfortunately is engaged tomorrow, but who solemnly commits himself for *Friday* [July 3]. I shall expect you then that day at the same place at

52 M. Beerbohm, *A Memory of Henry James and Joseph Conrad Conversing at an Afternoon Party—Circa 1904,* graphite and watercolor, 1924, Harry Ransom Humanities Research Center, University of Texas at Austin

53 F. Morellec, *Interior of Whistler's Former Studio, rue Notre-Dame-des-Champs,* photographed in 1994

the same hour (Reform Club, Pall Mall, 8 o'clock) in the hope that this will be just as convenient for you.—In the meantime, at *2 o'clock tomorrow,* we shall go to see all the Burne-Joneses and Rossettis possible. All my best to you.[4]

It is surprising that James should have proposed introducing Montesquiou to Whistler. The two Americans hardly consorted together in artistic London, and James had shown in print little esteem for his elder compatriot, who had been having such a beleagured time in London up until then. In 1877 James had written of Whistler's works shown at the Grosvenor Gallery: "Mr. Whistler's productions are, in the very nature of the case, uninteresting; they belong to the closet, not to the world." [5] His opinion was not to change much after that. But perhaps Montesquiou, who had certainly read about the Ruskin trial and the Peacock Room scandal, had asked to meet the artist.

Their first encounter seems to have been a success, as Montesquiou would recall many years later:

> I first met him...once when I set off to discover London, the Handel Festival, William Blake and William Morris, Alma Tadema, the "Pastorals" at Coombe, in short a whole esthetic salad, of which I immediately perceived that this same Whistler constituted the principal leaf.…The famous "Jimmie," whom we had seen in his studio, later received us at luncheon there, and prepared for us himself, with a chafing dish, some fried eggs, that represented, at that very moment, the most seductive of "arrangements" in white and yellow. He soon reduced to their just proportions, thanks to his elegant sarcasms, all that was not his in what we had come to admire; and I profited so well from the lesson, that, not too many years after, as I recall, when I posed for him, [it was] at least as much to realize the mysterious portrait, as to find again the mysterious painter.[6]

At the time of their first encounter at the Reform Club, Whistler was fifty-one years old, and Montesquiou thirty.

While in London, Montesquiou managed to see Whistler's Peacock Room at Frederick Leyland's house and, guided by Burne-Jones, visited the studio of William Morris, whose "Honeysuckle" pattern would soon be incorporated in the décor of Montesquiou's apartment on the quai d'Orsay. Passing through Paris in August on his way to Saint-Moritz, Montesquiou requested James' address from Polignac [7] and wrote a letter, to which James responded (in French):

> I am happy to know that you have preserved such a good memory of your all too brief visit to London, and send you this note to encourage you to return without fearing that your beautiful impressions be spoiled. I think that the interest you took in many things could only increase with a more intimate knowledge of them and that, for you as for all those who have finished by attaching themselves to English life, the first impression and the slightly lusterless exterior surface (of many elements) turn out to have been only a mask concealing the delights which await you. . . .[8]

54 J. S. Sargent, *Dr. Pozzi at Home,* oil, 1881, Los Angeles, U.C.L.A. at The Armand Hammer Museum of Art and Cultural Center

55 Whistler, *The Village Sweet Shop*,
etching, 1884–86, Art Institute of
Chicago

The only impression James noted of Montesquiou was that he had found
him "curious, but slight." [9]

Nearly two years passed before Montesquiou approached
Whistler again. On May 10, 1887, he reminded the artist that he had
promised to send an impression of his recent etching *The Village Sweet
Shop* (fig. 55), requested a photograph of Whistler, and addressed to him a
poem, composed soon after their first meeting, called *Fiat Nox et Fiat
Lux,* whose concluding lines read:

> *Toute la clarté—tout le mystère*
> *Près de tout l'obscur—de tout le clair:*
> *C'est la loi du Ciel et de la Terre*
> *Des créations du Dieu-Whistler.* [10]

Writing from the Beefsteak Club, Whistler thanked the poet for
his "masterpiece…so delicate," and sent off the etching, telling
Montesquiou how flattering it is for an artist to have his most recent work
selected for special praise. [11] In replying, the poet dropped the ceremonial
tone of his previous exchanges with Whistler and slipped into the
alliterative and punning mode that would characterize their subsequent
exchanges: "Nothing more mysterious, merry, inciting and inviting than
this pretty street stall 'of your invention'—and whose inventory would
be so difficult to inventorize." [12]

Another year would pass before an envelope sealed with
Montesquiou's characteristic silvered bat insignia (see title page) was
deposited on May 26 at Whistler's hotel in Paris—he was there to correct
proofs of the translation by Mallarmé (fig. 14) of his *Ten O'Clock*—
inviting the artist to view his collection of Japanese embroidered silks.
Though tempted, Whistler was eager to return to London. Instead, he
proposed luncheon to Montesquiou and offered to lead him on to an
exhibition of his most recent work at the Galerie Durand-Ruel. [13]

The following month found Montesquiou in London, residing at
13 Caroline Street, Bedford Square, and replying in Biblical terms to
Whistler's invitation to one of his celebrated "breakfasts" on Sunday,
July 1: "Keep awake, and pray, for I shall come amidst you like a thief in
the night—and at the moment when you expect him the least." [14] These
occasions, which brought together a mixture of Whistler's patrons,
followers, and distinguished visitors, were noted for the quality of
conversation, food, and drink proferred in the most refined of décors at
Whistler's residence in Chelsea. Whistler's "breakfasts"—they were set for
11:30 in the morning—could be considered the origin of the modern
"brunch."

The artist's marriage on August 11, 1888, to Beatrice Godwin
(1857–1896), widow of the architect Edward William Godwin, prompted
Montesquiou to send the couple as a wedding gift a tiny gold butterfly,
confected probably by René Lalique (fig. 56). When the Whistlers arrived
in Paris a few days later to begin their honeymoon, Montesquiou was
immediately informed of their presence: "…we await you all—I say 'all'
my dear friend because of the little butterfly made of gold and sunlight
that you caused to fly across the Channel to find us and which never
leaves us." [15]

Referring to the object now as a "Butterfly-God," Whistler wrote to Montesquiou early in 1889, assuring him that, "there is no one I want to see more than you." [16] The poet's response, dated February 10, is the first letter to allude to the possibility of a portrait of Montesquiou being painted by Whistler: "They are asking for my portrait for the Exposition Universelle: what a shame it was not yours." [17] Instead, the poet lent his portrait of 1879 by Lucien Doucet (fig. 21), which was shown as No. 484, *Portrait de M. R. de M.;* Doucet, who referred to the painting as "The Greyhound in the Fur-Lined Coat," also showed another work entitled *Five o'clock tea.*

On November 16, 1889, Montesquiou was writing Whistler again, this time thanking him for the gift of an etching the artist had executed at Loches the previous year (see fig. 57)—"the miraculous spider's web from Loches"—and telling him that the bonsai Montesquiou and his Japanese gardener had been cultivating for him "*was threatening to grow bigger!*" [18]

In December exchanges reversed direction, with Montesquiou sending Whistler, upon his urgent request, the red silk rosette of the Légion d'Honneur, to which the artist had just been named Chevalier. "Be kinder than ever, if that is possible," the artist wrote, "—and find me—*but immediately!* the little red ribbon, attached to its button, all ready for my buttonhole—The most delicate little ribbon, the most seductive that exists!" [19] Montesquiou soon sent him six of what he called "these red vermicelli," [20] and his cousin, now the Comtesse Greffulhe, joined in the festivities by offering Whistler a rosette made with her own hands. [21] The decoration is clearly indicated in Boldini's portrait of Whistler (fig. 15).

After another year marked by exchanges of correspondence, poems, and the newly published *Gentle Art of Making Enemies,* Montesquiou finally proposed commissioning his portrait from Whistler, even bringing up the delicate subject of payment, in a letter postmarked February 13, 1891:

> No, what would more likely bring me your way would be to *make a step toward your palette.* It is to see and to know and to have and to appreciate...*the graphic corollary,* the *figurative, indispensible, unique evidence,* and the *consecrating* commentary on *what I intend to leave after me in the way of glory*—along with a little interest on your part, I think. Some rather well-intentioned and oracular friends have had the prophetic and sensitive sense to draw my attention recently again on this prestigious point, which was already concentrated on it *theoretically,* but when will take place *the application,* the *getting to work,* and on a *masterwork, on canvas,* and *in the frame?*...And so and more eloquently and eulogistically have the friendly voices reasoned reasonably, which dislodged me from my *fatalistic anticipation* and *hope*—and made me *count some coins!*...
> I propose—you dispose! [22]

Aware of Montesquiou's powerful associations in Paris, and perhaps touched by his enthusiasm and generous nature—the poet had just sent Beatrice Whistler two jewelled pins in the form of butterflies—Whistler committed himself to the project in March, writing the poet:

56 French, *Butterfly,* gold and glass, 1888,
Glasgow, Hunterian Art Gallery

Come, you glib talker! All will be told during the posing
sessions....So—all is prepared, as you can see, for our masterpiece!—and this time it is serious, so much so that I scarcely dare
speak of it!—and so be prepared to spend some time in this
country of tranquil climate! until the end of our great undertaking, no?...One word—See you again soon—my dear bat! [23]

Work on the portrait seems to have begun in Whistler's new
studio at 21 Cheyne Walk in March 1891, soon after Montesquiou sent the
artist this message: "And the bat will flit toward you at the five o'clock
sunset." [24] However, prior to the establishment of the portrait's format and
pose, Montesquiou had attempted to influence Whistler's decision on
these matters by having the Comtesse Greffulhe—whose beauty, wealth,
and social prestige had already dazzled Whistler—make a few suggestions
to the artist, suggestions which, of course, reflected Montesquiou's own
thoughts. In a hitherto unpublished letter, Montesquiou wrote his cousin:

> I hope that your letter that I asked you to write to my butterfly
> is ready and should have *a so pressing and powerful influence*
> on his aerial tricks. Don't make me wait for it, and if by chance
> you should be held up, write it straight from your imagination....
> The model also asks to be reinflated...but [he is] terror-stricken at
> the awful idea that came to you, that it might happen that one
> extract "*a* chic *little young man*" out of the form of a fallen but
> unconquered archangel. [25]

Writing on March 16, the Comtesse rose spiritedly to the
occasion, attempting to convince Whistler to depict her cousin in his
preferred profile view:

> I congratulate you on the *tremendous event* that is about to take
> place in your studio, for he whose portrait you are about to
> execute is great too and will live through your work and his
> own—an indissoluble exchange. It is rare that a painter finds a
> model—the contrary is just as rare. In the present circumstance,
> doesn't it seem that this encounter was destined over centuries?
> This unique vision must be unique—Take a long time in
> selecting the pose. Before someone so complex, doesn't one have
> to fight against a thousand temptations—He has, among other
> things, an expression which must be captured and which is
> the medium through which his personality is revealed and where
> his soulfulness conforms to his interior being. You must be
> careful not to be too quickly seduced by the extreme elegance of
> his class. I would tremble to see a "Robert de Montesquiou" as a
> "chic young man from the end of the nineteenth century" (which
> he can be too)—You would like to see him full face; and you
> would be right! I should like the profile and I would be right!—
> The "very beautiful profile" carved by Michelangelo with the
> intensity of the eye that *sees* and that *thinks,*—in contrast to those
> who look without seeing, and who, even more, have never
> thought. But, I observe, my dear Master, that I am in the process
> of giving you a lesson! And so I take my leave in haste in order
> to await the results.[26]

Confronting the Montesquiou-Greffulhe forces, Whistler obviously
followed his own inclinations concerning the pose and depicted his
subject full-face.

Montesquiou seems to have kept himself in London available for posing steadily from March through May of 1891.[27] The surviving correspondence from this period includes a sly reference by Whistler to the Comtesse Greffulhe—"Let us get together this tranquil Sunday, to continue the picture that la Belle Dame à grand merci awaits in its perfection—and which I do not yet dare to offer you"[28]—and occasional references to the artist's cancelling appointments, such as a note sent in March that commences, "Bat, dear Bat! the Butterflies are inconsolable and invisible tomorrow!" and ends with a piquant detail: "What an awful reception we offer our friend incognito."[29] In fact, Montesquiou had taken elaborate trouble to pass unnoticed during his stay in London, as Graham Robertson recorded with amusement:

> He was in England incognito (I cannot imagine why) and took such delight in gliding down unfrequented ways and adopting strange aliases: visiting me by stealth after dusk with an agreeable suggestion of dark lanterns and disguise cloaks, though, as he was almost unknown in London, he might have walked at noon down Piccadilly accompanied by a brass band without anyone being much the wiser; Whistler, who also loved to play at secrets, was equally clandestine; I dutifully acting under orders, dissembled energetically, and Montesquiou was so wrapped about in thick mystery that no intelligent acquaintance within the three mile radius could possibly have failed to notice him.[30]

During this spring of 1891, Montesquiou occasionally threatened to return to Paris, thus stirring Whistler to action, as suggested by a card the artist mailed in April:

> Very dear friend—your charming letter, which is a rose surprise—and, as always, a poem—saddened us all because it makes us once again think of your departure—But since you want to reassure us, I am going to demonstrate to you my new-found courage, by borrowing from the promised quarter hours, all day tomorrow.

It continues in a fashion difficult to interpret fully, but which suggests the complexities into which the portrait project had fallen: "Yes, let us leave to mellow in its mystery the Black Knight—and pray for some rays from the poor sun of this Chelsea in mourning for the masterpieces marked with craquelures and await Thursday to continue—These delays have always led to success with me!"[31] The reference to "masterpieces" and to "the Black Knight" in particular lends credence to the tradition that Whistler was working on two different versions of Montesquiou's portrait, a possibility suggested in a letter Montesquiou sent Whistler on May 6, stating that "a second round...will treat us better."[32]

On July 7, 1891, Montesquiou's role model, Edmond de Goncourt, visited his acolyte's apartment on the rue Franklin and noted in his diary another corroboration of the existence of two portraits:

> When I stopped in front of a Whistler etching, Montesquiou told me that Whistler was doing two portraits of him at the moment: one in evening dress with a fur over his arm, and the other in a long grey coat with the collar turned up and, at the neck, a little nothing of a tie of a nuance, of a nuance...which he did not specify but which the expression in his eyes indicated was the ideal hue. And Montesquiou was very interesting on the subject

of the painting technique used by Whistler, to whom he gave seventeen sittings during a month's stay in London....Oh! sittings in which it seemed to Montesquiou that Whistler, with his fixed attention, was emptying him of life, was "pumping away" something of his individuality; and afterwards he used to feel so exhausted that his whole body was unutterably tense, and he felt thankful to have discovered a certain *coca* wine which restored his energy after those dreadful sittings.[33]

De Goncourt's "long grey coat" portrait would correspond to one a journalist named Saint-Charles referred to in his article "Un Tableau de Whistler," published in *Le Figaro* on November 27, 1891:

> And if I didn't fear being indiscreet, I would tell the story of an unfinished portrait of the Comte de...which should be called *Impressions of Pearl Grey,* and for which the model had to spend months in London and at Brighton, awaiting with Whistler a grey light that didn't come! And Whistler who has never given in since his birth...will not give in. The portrait will not be completed until the day the light is pearl grey. [34]

Though the fate of this version of Montesquiou's portrait has long seemed uncertain—MacDonald even wondered whether it might have been painted over for the surviving "Black Knight" portrait—Whistler wrote Montesquiou of its status quite clearly in 1894: "It is *splendid* the real Dartagnan!—and the false one has disappeared... in a thousand pieces!" Furthermore, X-ray studies of the Frick painting made at The Metropolitan Museum of Art in 1994 revealed no significant compositional differences beneath the paint surface.[35]

From this same period of May-June 1891 dates a letter Beatrice Whistler wrote to Montesquiou alluding to a significant aspect of the artist's working methods: "However, my invalid is getting rapidly better, and will be ready in a few days to finish the 'Black Lord' if you will come back and help him. You have no idea how splendid he is in the new frame! Come and see?" [36] Not only had the artist already procured a frame for the unfinished portrait—from Frederick Henry Grau of 570 Fulton Road, his usual framer (see fig. 58)—but he was working on the canvas in its frame (see frontispiece). Arthur Jerome Eddy (1859–1920), the Chicago lawyer and collector of contemporary art, could corroborate this practice as the result of posing for Whistler in 1894: "After the first few days he would place the canvas in its frame, and thereafter paint with it so." Eddy also quoted Whistler's explanation for working this way, a habit he might have picked up from his early teacher, Charles Gleyre:

> The one aim of the unsuspecting painter is to make his man "stand out" from the frame, never doubting that, on the contrary, he should really, and in truth absolutely does, stand *within* the frame, and at a depth behind it equal to the distance at which the painter sees his model. The frame is, indeed, the window through which the painter looks at his model, and nothing could be more offensively inartistic than this brutal attempt to thrust the model on the hitherside of this window. [37]

Finally, the fact that Whistler was continually working on the black portrait in its gilded frame may explain the mystifying title he gave the finished work, *Arrangement in Black and Gold: Comte Robert de*

57 Whistler, *Renaissance Window, Loches*, etching, 1888, Art Institute of Chicago

Montesquiou-Fezensac, for there is not a trace of gold within the picture.

In June 1891, Whistler was in Paris and seeing a lot of Montesquiou, but not yet working on the portrait there, as he wrote to his wife on the 14th:

> He thinks that the return to the portrait must be in September— about—So the great sums must be coming from other sources in our good fortune—Well—upon the whole I daresay it is just as well—I confess I am rather relieved...if we have warm weather doubtless we should be couped up with the black portrait and perhaps a little bored—etc? [38]

The theme of payment here for the first time sounds as a minor chord.

Montesquiou returned to his obsession with secrecy in all that concerned the portrait when he wrote to Whistler in London that same month:

> The mutual concern for our work, your enlightened coquetry about your masterpieces, our light-hearted and reciprocal conscientiousness about the future and final apotheosis of our precious and gracious and glorious cooperation, make me propose to you the discreet suggestion (which will make you smile secretly in two days!)—not to expose even the corner of either of our prestigious and prodigious(!) schemes [another possible reference to the existence of two versions of the portrait]...for the benefit of any visitor coming from Paris—with no *exception!*—sic. Play the innocent: *that suits you so well!* [39]

While Whistler generally respected Montesquiou's desire for secrecy, he could not resist showing the portrait to Monet when the latter passed through London early in 1892.

On October 10, Whistler wrote to Montesquiou of the difficulties he encountered trying to work on the portrait at a time when other problems were confronting him, most notably his lawsuit against Sheridan Ford, who, without the artist's permission, had published in Belgium an edition of *The Gentle Art of Making Enemies:*

> What can we do, my friend?…I must be at Antwerp on the 24th of the month, so that I can appear [at court] on the appointed day—That is still a bit off—and we would really have the time to finish the "mystery" that awaits you—but there would be inter- ruptions.…I just turned around the picture that implores us to finish it!—But the few days necessary must be completely without bother—without preoccupations. Unless you came at the end of next week, then we could get to work on Saturday— (a week from today) [October 17]—I would leave for Antwerp Saturday the 24th, and if the canvas is not absolutely completed, as it really should be—you would make a little trip to the countryside, and I would be back for Tuesday [October 27]. [40]

In view of what still lay ahead, the artist seemed remarkably positive at this date about his progress with the work, but Montesquiou declined to come over to London—ostensibly because of the fog.

Having put his affairs in order by the fall, Whistler was able to write Montesquiou in early November: "I send you these two words to let you know that all is ready," [41] to which the poet responded on November 8: ". . . I shall brave the only [mystery] that can really mystify us, that is

58 F. H. Grau, *Signature on frame of Whistler's Portrait of Montesquiou*, 1891, New York, Frick Collection

the *Mist* in person; which perhaps, priding itself at not impeding so precious a project, will do us the honor of allowing itself to *demist* and disappear."[42] In the same letter, Montesquiou spoke of bringing to London "a certain heavy and light burden" that turned out to be his long poem *Moth,* which he composed in Whistler's honor following the news that the French government had offered to buy the latter's *Arrangement in Grey and Black: Portrait of the Painter's Mother* (fig. 10).

Making specific references in the poem to many of the artist's works, including all those in The Frick Collection today—the etchings and pastels executed in Venice in 1879–80 (see figs. 12, 13), *The Ocean* (fig. 5), *Mrs. Frederick R. Leyland, Miss Rosa Corder* (fig. 123), and *Lady Meux*—Montesquiou twice evoked some of his own experiences in posing for Whistler:

> *Car sa touche se puise au sein vrai de la vie;*
> *Pas un trait ne s'empreint hormis que bien vital,*
> *Et notre lassitude à poser est suivie*
> *D'un lever de nous-mêmes au cadre de métal!*
>
> *Ces yeux que nul n'a fait voir comme en tes peintures;*
> *Les yeux du deuil des nuits, ces yeux du seuil des jours;*
> *Ces yeux auxquels tu dis, dans la pose qui dure*
> *Regardez-moi ce peu, pour regarder toujours!*[43]

The last line alludes to a dramatic moment during Montesquiou's posing that the poet recalled in his memoirs at the conclusion of his chapter on Whistler:

> And so, apparently having provoked in the portrait the encounter of Poe's Wilson with his *doppelgänger,* of Shelley's Zoroaster with himself, or of Musset with the "young man dressed in black, who resembled him like a brother," such an apparition made the artist exclaim to me in a triumphant cry this phrase, perhaps the most beautiful of all ever spoken by a painter: "Look at me for an instant longer, AND YOU WILL LOOK FOREVER!"[44]

Montesquiou went on to recall that by the end of his reading of the poem to Whistler, "the emotion that this terribly sensitive but pent-up man allowed to show gave me one of the highest rewards for my efforts that I have been permitted to receive over the course of this life."[45] *Moth* was published in *Les Chauves-Souris* in 1892.

Of greater interest for posterity than the labored stanzas of *Moth* were the notes concerning Whistler that Montesquiou put down after his posing sessions and eventually had published in his memoirs many years later. While most of these pages are devoted to the retelling of some of the artist's more familiar jibes, some are subtly fresh, as in his comparison of Whistler to "a rare bird, whose egret would be his tuft of white hair, whose brilliant little eyes are like jet beads, [with] a hooked beak, a round tongue, continually whirling around in its strident socket, and whose cries would be some '*bons mots.*'"[46] In this context, it is interesting that Helleu's daughter Paulette recalled Montesquiou's voice as sounding "like the cry of a peacock, clearly audible three rooms away."[47]

Also, few of Whistler's subjects left as vivid a record of what it was like to pose for the artist.

What became of my personal image [Montesquiou asked rhetorically] throughout these beautiful tales that alternated with the poses? It progressed by intermittent leaps of posing sessions sometimes consecutive, sometimes separated by more or less long intervals. Occasionally, it seemed to slow down, to pull back, to go off into shadows, as the result of a fundamental law of this peculiar art that seemed close to sorcery.

"It's all buzzing up there, the canvas isn't satisfied yet . . .," he would exclaim, punctuating his words with "that's it" as he accelerated his work during the first nearly frenetic sessions during which he behaved like a tiger just let out of his cage, to such a point that it was necessary to have all the furniture removed to prevent the artist from falling over backwards as he leapt around, when he would pull back, one might say, to draw a look from the very essence of the model, and convey it onto the canvas without giving it the time to evaporate or vanish.…The very last sessions are carried out in much the same fashion in order to obtain what the Master calls "the easy look of the thing." Between these two points of departure and arrival, the innumerable and interminable posing sessions (I posed more than a hundred times) are like drills during which the painting, "done before lunch," seems to submit to the very laws of human growth.

Let us not forget that my portrait was, no doubt, the last full-length figure that Whistler painted [*sic*]; perhaps his hand and, as a result, his touch, were beginning to feel less sure, to hesitate a bit; it is possible, although the final result shows nothing of it; but it seems to me that this unique spectacle that I witnessed must always have characterized his manner, I mean that curious way of pulling back, of balancing the stroke, of letting it wander in the air for prolonged moments before setting it down at the precise spot where the work needed it, in order to approach even closer to the heartbeat, the breath of life. Let us not forget either that this man said, of the work of art worthy of the name, that it should be executed the way nature produces plants, and must represent a long, slow addition derived bit by bit from all the artist could deduct of the impalpable from reality, in order to set the sum.

But, since this demanding situation could, at any moment, become another that one had never dreamt of, a rather exacting obligation for the model resulted, an obligation to reappear and to hold up, each time, in the initial costume and in the original pose, if he wished to collaborate conscientiously in the creation of his own effigy. Impossible, from this point on, to show oneself less up to these conditions than the woman who thought she really could, before such a man, have her chambermaid pose in her mistress' garments; such a way of understanding the rendering of nature and the recording of character always seems less than intelligent.

Oddly enough, as we shall see, both Montesquiou and Whistler would be guilty of playing this trick of using substitute models. The memoirs continue in an increasingly interpretive vein:

69

…but, in Whistler's case, it was the absolute negation of his "technique"; never was the execution of a painting more removed from a brush and artistic tricks, for a painter who seemed always to say "*surge et veni!*" [rise and come forward] to the resemblance being formed—I was going to say being fermented—in his mysterious alchemy. This pursued resemblance, one would have said Whistler extracted it from the canvas rather than putting it upon it, or rather that there was something of the two prodigies in its final apparition, definitively set upon the surface that awaited it.[48]

Arthur Jerome Eddy (fig. 59), who was posing for Whistler at this time, also noted his impressions of the experience—impressions that both corroborate and go beyond those of Montesquiou:

Once inside his studio, Whistler seemed to lose all the eccentricities of manner by which he was known to the world. He doffed his coat, substituted for his monocle a pair of serviceable spectacles, and was ready for work. If it were a full-length portrait, he placed the canvas near his palette and his sitter in pose about four feet to the other side of the easel. For observation he stood about twelve feet back towards the doorway….The light fell slanting on the right of the portrait and sitter, over the painter's left shoulder, and this light he would modify each day according to the amount of sunshine and the effect he desired.…

Eddy, like Montesquiou, recalled Whistler's transferring his visual impressions to the canvas "with a run and a slide," but Eddy had a sharper eye than Montesquiou's for noting the technical procedures the artist followed:

He worked with great rapidity and long hours, but he used his colors thin and covered the canvas with innumerable coats of paint. The colors increased in depth and intensity as the work progressed. At first the entire figure was painted in grayish-brown tones, with very little of flesh color, the whole blending perfectly with the grayish-brown of the prepared canvas; then the entire background would be intensified a little; then the figure made a little stronger; then the background, and so on from day to day and week to week, and often from month to month, to the exhaustion of the sitter, but the perfection of the work, if the sitter remained patient and continued in favor. At no time did he permit the figure to get away from or out of the background; at no time did he permit the background to oppress the figure, but the development of both was even and harmonious, with neither discord nor undue contrast.

Eddy concluded his report much as Montesquiou had his, both of them seeing Whistler as a magician: "It was as if the portrait were hidden within the canvas and the master by passing his wands day after day over the surface evoked the image." [49]

During late November and early December of 1891, Whistler teased Montesquiou with some hesitant progress on the portrait, as suggested by this note: "Until tomorrow, my dear friend—we shall lunch, we shall chat, and—perhaps we shall continue!" [50] But to Mallarmé, Whistler described progress on the portrait as relentless, all the while

59 Whistler, *Arrangement in Flesh Color and Brown: Portrait of Arthur J. Eddy,* oil, 1894, Art Institute of Chicago

beseeching the poet not to talk of it: "Now my dear friend I shall tell you why my letters are always late—You know that Montesquiou is here—and I work on the portrait every day into the night—and so every evening I miss the mail—You know this is absolutely *between ourselves*—and you will not say anything to anyone about this new picture, no?" [51]

Just before his return to Paris in December, Montesquiou seemed sufficiently convinced that the end was in sight to say so—and, more importantly, to raise again the matter of payment:

> My dear Master! I do not wish to leave this land of *mystery* and of *mist* where our glorious happiness was fortunately overlaid with some sufferings without which there is neither pleasure nor well-being, without entrusting to the *written word* some of the deep feelings of gratitude of which the *spoken word* occasionally fears not striking the atmosphere in a worthy fashion.
> You will carry me off in your own glory to immortality, where mine certainly intends, one day, to serve yours in turn amongst contemplations in the future that will unite the names of the Painter and the Poet.
> *I therefore thank you.* And that is, after all, even perhaps before all, the most beautiful word, when it is well said.
> Now the moment has come to remind you of your old expression: "Let us wait until we have made something really beautiful, and then, you will send me a large coin." The something really beautiful now *existing,* the *large* thing asks to have its size established. Write to me therefore no less and no more than if I were a *simple minister of fine arts....* [52]

Whistler indeed wrote back to "Monsieur le Ministre," but he evaded the question of payment: "Any coin would be far too big in this atmosphere of fog—and at this moment—It will be in Paris midst the joy and the sunlight of completion that the picture which has given you so much trouble will be delivered—And you will know...that it is only after the official hanging that we can turn to the Budget." [53]

The artist disliked mixing business with the mysteries of creation, as he wrote in 1901 to the future owner of Montesquiou's portrait, Richard A. Canfield (fig. 74), who had boldly sent the artist a check for "certain pictures not completed":

> You have seen that the work is all absorbing—and indeed I myself find the difficulties in the brush quite sufficient in themselves, without allowing them to become complicated with anything distantly resembling responsibility of any kind!...
> You will remember that I received your first cheque without hesitation—sympathising entirely with the spirit in which it was sent—I think it will not be at all difficult for you, who have so far shown such ready understanding, to see with me, that this is as much of a link with business as I can stand in the midst of incompleted work. [54]

Writing Whistler on New Year's Eve of 1891 from the château of Charnizay, Montesquiou reported enthusiastically that he had made arrangements for the artist to utilize part of the studio of Antonio de La Gandara to complete the portrait in Paris, where Whistler as yet had no studio of his own:

60 F. Morellec, *Courtyard of 22 rue Monsieur-le-Prince,* photographed in 1994

Therefore in the event that the project of "*the G studio*" should still be agreeable to you, the absence of the painter [Joseph-Félix Bouchor, see below] at precisely that time will make the thing even easier.…So tell me what you finally decide, so that I can warn the said G who will not leave until he has received *the sacred box* [presumably the crate containing the portrait] and installed it smoothly and without damage in *the consecrated studio.* Talk to me also *about dates,* so that I can be available.

He concluded with the familiar call for secrecy:

Useless to add to your subtle wariness and guidance the important and sine qua non condition for success and final (and *foxy*) crowning of our *immortal venture;* to wit *absolute secrecy* and *without exception* during these last brushstrokes in Paris. Envious ingratitude and jealous mediocrity *quaerentes quem devorent* [looking for whom they might devour] would not miss trying to take something away, and would perhaps succeed at least in sickening us with their odious spectacle.…[55]

La Gandara's studio was located at 22 rue Monsieur-le-Prince (fig. 60), near the place de l'Odéon. The portion of it that he was offering Whistler was a room on the second floor facing the courtyard, space that was normally occupied by Joseph-Félix Bouchor (1853–1937), a landscapist and painter of genre scenes who would receive a second-class medal at the Salon of 1892. The building, with its imposing entrance portal ornamented with sculpture, was designed specifically for studios. Among other artists who occupied them were three Americans: Wilburg Winfield Woodward (living there in 1879), Philip Leslie Hale (there between 1888 and 1890), and the latter's sister Ellen Day Hale (in 1890). La Gandara would die in this building in 1917, as attested by a stone plaque at the entrance.[56]

Bouchor graciously relinquished his space to Whistler, but initially for a brief time only:

Monsieur de La Gandara has told me that it would be agreeable to you to continue your portrait in my studio—I am pleased therefore, Monsieur, to be able to place it at your disposition for the week that I shall remain away. You can occupy it beginning tomorrow. I was very touched, Monsieur, by your words of thanks. Believe me that it is a great honor for me and a great pleasure to have you as a guest for several days.

Whistler later turned over this letter to Montesquiou, with a note in the margin: "What cheek—sublime!" in reference to Bouchor's use of the phrase "my studio," even though it did not belong to him.[57] From such a start, it is not surprising that Whistler's relations with Bouchor should have become strained, as suggested by the way the former spoke of him to Montesquiou at the end of February: "our friend the enemy." [58]

And so it was to the landlord La Gandara that Whistler addressed his special thanks for the loan of the space, in the form of a table palette that he asked his wife to order in London, appending a tiny drawing of the palette to his letter (fig. 61):

Now one thing most important—you must send for Grau [Whistler's framer] and tell him to make at once, a palette exactly like mine—the same size etc.…with the little boxes all round for the paints—you know—finish it at once—pack it up and send it to Monsieur de La Gandara, 22 rue Monsieur le Prince, Paris. He went on to evoke the tone of his relationship with La Gandara: "I cannot tell you how courteous and kind he has been—nor can I exagerate the unheard of trouble I have given him—Happily this present from me will be for him a joy beyond all past annoyances—and I am sure you will wish him to have it…." [59] Whistler's palette (fig. 62) was described by Montesquiou as "a huge mahogany table in the corner of which, on a minuscule silver plaque, flits the *butterfly*," [60] and by Eddy as "a rectangular table that resembled a writing-desk. The top sloped slightly; at the left were tubes of colors, at the right one or two bowls containing oil and turpentine, with which the colors when mixed were reduced so thin that they would run on the sloping top of the table." [61]

While Montesquiou was posing with some regularity in Paris during January and February of 1892, few letters were exchanged with the artist, but Whistler kept his wife informed of his progress—or lack of it. This time it was primarily Montesquiou's social involvements that were interfering with the completion of the portrait. Whistler, who told him that such preoccupations were "*pour les Madames,*" would try to lure him to the studio with practical arguments: "Everything is set!—and we begin on *Tuesday*—at *one* o'clock, no? I should have the background prepared before you arrive—so that we can continue immediately—but then you cannot let me down, or the 'material' would have dried—and the enamelled effect lost!" [62] The final phrase—"*et l'émail serait perdu*"—is one of the few surviving indications of Whistler's technical intentions with the work. At this time he apparently sought such a transparent surface effect more than once, for another sitter, John James Cowan, remembered Whistler saying of his portrait in 1895: "It is devilish pretty. This will be an enamel if it is nothing else." And at least one critic who viewed Montesquiou's portrait in 1894 commented on Whistler's achievement in this regard: "Tarnished black enamel might describe the beauty of the execution attained by the painter in the rendering of the dusky surrounding." [63]

Before setting off to Paris to complete the portrait, Whistler had been optimistic, writing Montesquiou: "Let us hope!…I was there this morning to look at the beautiful picture which asks of me only a few hours to come to life." [64] Once in the capital, however, the artist was more uncertain, as he wrote to his wife: "The work itself is supposed to begin tomorrow—and *perhaps* all may go well." [65]

Another letter to Beatrice, mailed on January 28, sums up the artist's frustrations:

Poor Mallarmé I have seen—and I went again to his evening on Tuesday—only too glad to get away from an atmosphere of "respectueux"!—which by the way I may as well say that I should not be in the least depressed by were I not all the while conscious of this everlasting great work—with which, by dint of long dragging, this melancholy "triste et noble" one [Montesquiou] has become *entirely too intimate!* It is doubtless that [which] demoralises me—and makes me fancyful and suspicious in his excellent company!—And now tomorrow he has insisted upon my going to a matinée at the Vaudeville where they are going to play away a whole hurrah of Wagner! and this in the middle of the day when I wanted to be at my painting! Of course all Paris—and of course the Gréfülhe—and the Countess de What's her name you know we met her at the Exposition—and so I am to drag my well-cut and well-worn rags accross the water and seat myself in the stall in the…afternoon!—And you know how I shall hate it!—and all because of this great black work that still is there—an eternal terror and reproach until it is done!—However I am not *sure* that it may not come out right after all. . . .[66]

The concert outing the following day ended on a happy note for the artist, as he wrote Beatrice:

> Directly the Concert finished, Madame Grefhüle, the Count of course, and a whole banquet of Princes go over to Goupils! [Whistler's Paris gallery] and sit for *two hours*.…They look at the pastels and the little landscape and admire the lithographs and altogether the whole thing amazing!—un succès colossale! to be spread all over Paris in the next few hours as Montesquiou said—and who was enchanted!

However, earlier in the same letter of January 31, Whistler had described his slow progress with the portrait in discouraged tones:

> Of course things here are endless—and the complications without termination! Each day something.…So that the work itself is not really properly got at—In the first I was only installed in the studio of Gandara's friend on Tuesday night—The next day, *Wednesday* I had an afternoon with Montesquiou—very *quiet*—and doing I believe a great deal of good to *the head*—well then as I told you he announced that the Friday had to be given up to the 'World'—whereupon I made up my mind that I would not touch the background and figure until *afterwards* for I was determined to go through with the whole picture in *one* perfect final coating—for which I had been enabled to prepare the canvas with one last scraping and poummice stoning and washing and the terrible bag of tricks that we know only too well!

Then Bouchor returned unexpectedly and required his studio, much to Whistler's annoyance, as conveyed at the end of this same letter: "So that again no chance of beginning—again the unfortunate black work toiled with and struggled back into its box—to be kept in hiding until this newcomer [Bouchor] shall have got himself away into the Country again!—Isn't it terrible?" [67]

One means of gaining time that Whistler found was to have La Gandara pose in Montesquiou's place, a convenient ruse inasmuch as the Spaniard was tall, thin, and handsome like the count. Whistler reported to Beatrice:

> Gandara is an excellent fellow—and devoted to me—Together we combined—and without a word I got him this morning to come and stand for me before the arrival of the Count!!—He brought his dress clothes and I put in the whole of the background and the tone of the figure—then he bolted and at about one o'clock Montesquiou appeared, and I put him in his place and went right on without his dreaming that another mortal had desecrated the atmosphere of the "respectueux" so necessary to

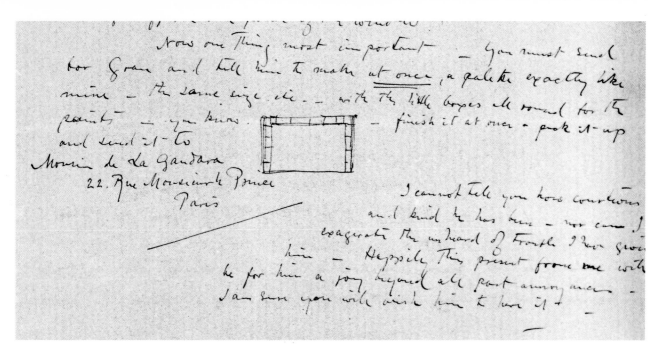

61 Whistler, *Letter to Beatrice Whistler*
(excerpt), January 1892, Glasgow
University Library

his existence!—Not bad was it Chinkie—However after all as he
explained to me this evening with some elaboration, Gandara
himself, de la Gandara is "of race"—born in short—so that after
all everything was saved! The picture tonight looked *superb!* [68]

The American writer Logan Pearsall Smith (1865–1946) recalled
having posed in Montesquiou's place as well. The vivid record he left of
the experience, joined with Montesquiou's and Eddy's memories of posing
for Whistler, greatly enhances our understanding of just how the portrait
came to be:

This nobleman [Montesquiou] was depicted in an aristocratic
pose, standing with a fur coat on his arm, and could not be
expected to give the almost innumerable sessions which Whistler
demanded of his subjects; but I could be easily called in to act as
his substitute in certain aspects of his appearance. I was, like him,
tall and slim, and could competently stand there with what was
the principal feature of the picture, the fur coat, flung across the
arm. I was pleased to oblige the great painter, I was delighted to
enjoy his company and watch him paint; but the task was one
of the most arduous I have ever undertaken. Whistler had not the
slightest pity for his subjects; art was something sacred, and the
sufferings of those in its service were a matter of complete
indifference to him. If, when he had finished his portraits of his
sitters, they should all perish, what could that have mattered
to the world?…But to die in the effort to make immortal the fur
coat of a stranger seemed to me a somewhat excessive sacrifice;

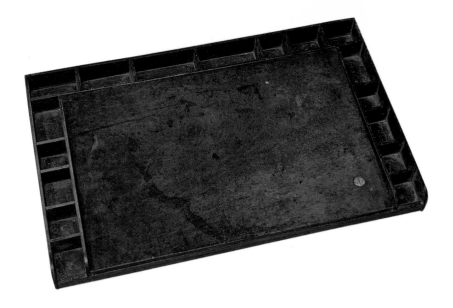

and when I had stood there until I felt I should die if I stood
there longer, and would beg for a little rest or some change of
position, "In a moment, in just a moment," Whistler would
cheerfully answer, and then would go on painting. His method,
as I observed it, was first of all to arrange his subject with incred-
ible pains and care, so that every detail was to his liking, and to
paint it with infinite touches and retouches; and then, when it
seemed finished and perfect in execution, to stand back, gaze at
it, and cry "Ha!" and rush at it in a kind of fury and paint the
whole thing out. It was like an actor rehearsing a part over and
over again till he gets it perfect; the final performance, which may
take a minute, has been preceded by many hours of rehearsal.
This was the case, I think even with Whistler's life-size portraits.
The actual painting of each, as we now see it, was performed in
the briefest of periods, but these had been preceded by an almost
infinite number of rehearsals.[69]

What Pearsall Smith called the "fur coat" in the portrait—an
item that Montesquiou found increasingly tiring to bear while posing—
was in fact a chinchilla cape belonging to the Comtesse Greffulhe, who
lent it so that she might be included symbolically in her adoring cousin's
portrait. For the artist, the subtle grey coloring of the fur introduced a
crucial relief from the stark black-and-white scheme of the portrait;
he utilized it much like the grey coat in the portrait of F. R. Leyland
(fig. 122), or the pink cloak in that of Théodore Duret (fig. 115).

During February 1892, Whistler continued to pretend that the portrait needed only a few finishing touches, luring Montesquiou back to the studio with arch references to one of his substitute models:

Now I see what was lacking in our picture—again "just in time"—to give it the dash and the perfect finish that it should possess before it is ready for its future!…Come tomorrow at two o'clock—even before—and—this a bit à la Gandara—pose as a proud poet and great friend, without looking at the canvas until the session is over.…Your terrible Painter.[70]

Montesquiou promptly responded to his "dear *Tyrant*," venting rather forcefully his frustrations:

You know that I am, at once, more and less *resigned* than Gandara *without its showing*. You hold me on a rather short leash; and to know the day before that I am free the next day would be useful for certain appointments. But *to obey you* is sweet for someone who has never done anything *but decide;* for this first and last example of my submission, admit that I chose well. You who have even better placed yours in the hands of your noble and beautiful Omphale [Beatrice], you will get your turn the day when it will please her, I tell you in all truth, that you *cease not finishing,* that which is already, and [has been] for a long time *Endless!*[71]

Though there would be subsequent alterations to the portrait, it apparently seemed to both Montesquiou and Whistler sufficiently finished by February 1892 for presentation to the sitter's cousin the Comtesse Albertine de Montebello (see fig. 29), a scene the artist described excitedly to his wife (fig. 64):

He is enchanted!—and this evening he went upstairs and brought down Madame de Montebello, who was standing for her picture to Gandara, poor fellow—I was not displeased that he should do so, for the whole picture had not yet sunk in—and the background and the figure all went beautifully together—Chinkie I wish you could have seen the two in front of the work!—They were splendid! these two amazing ones—all "respectueux" and absolutely without a doubt!—a sort of unveilling in Olympus— or last tableau in a very superior pantomime! Montesquiou was of course simply heroic—"triste et noble"—and childlike in his joy—It really was without precedent—in my experience—for *expression* of such sympathy is unknown to me hitherto—and impossible in England—Not that there was anything loud or accentuated even in their demonstration, but they gloried in the picture as an apotheosis of themselves, their birth their "race"!— "It is the acme of pride" said the Count, "untain[t]ed with vanity"!! "C'est *noble*" said the grande dame with a sort of religious intonation—and there they were really worshipping before a sort of *monument* of their blue blood!—Well you know Chinkie no more intoxicating recognition could possibly be offered the Wams [the Whistlers] than such an appreciation as this—I dare scarcely believe that the picture can be as superbe as in the gloaming it looked—You know how the poor grinder is lonely and timid in the morning—and how he lives in terror of the first peep at his painting before breakfast—Meanwhile however there is no doubt that Madame de Montebello looked at the portrait in its highest sense of achievement—no little thoughts of detail—no wishing for more of this or less of that—no desire for anything other—simply a supreme acceptation of the whole as the highest possible incarnation of all that is beautiful and dignified and magnificent—"C'est splendide!" she told Gandara when she went back to that sad Spaniard—un chef d'oeuvre!—and certainly in the flattering light of the evening our Montesquiou poète et grand seigneur did look stupendious! [72]

"In the gloaming" and "in the flattering light of evening" are key allusions in this great letter to the vision Whistler had had of the portrait all along, as suggested by his famous statement:

As the light fades and the shadows deepen, all petty and exacting details vanish, everything trivial disappears, and I see things as they are in great strong masses: the buttons are lost, but the garment remains; the garment is lost, but the sitter remains; the sitter is lost, but the shadow remains; the shadow is lost, but the picture remains. And *that,* night cannot efface from the painter's imagination. [73]

Eddy explained how Whistler went about this reductive procedure at that time:

And it was his habit to paint when the studio was filled with gloom and lengthening shadows crept across the floor; when it was so dark the dull eye of sitter or chance visitor could scarce distinguish the figure on the canvas. This "painting in the dark," as some have called it, was a singular trait. He would paint with increasing force and effect as the room became darker and darker, until it seemed as if the falling of night was an inspiration. [74]

That the Comtesse de Montebello's enthusiasm for the portrait was genuine and lasting is attested to by this letter she sent her cousin: "If you have a photograph of your magnificent portrait, send it to me. A work of such power is a *lesson,* for its creator has penetrated to the deepest crypts of true knowledge of a human being." [75]

But however great Whistler's satisfaction with the portrait might have been, he required assurances from Beatrice about it. He nervously wrote from London to her in Paris on March 15:

Tell me more about *the* picture. Is it *really* beautiful—What do you regret—is it only quickly to finish each little portion—that's easy—Is the great stature all right? Nothing absurd? or weak or worried or exaggerated in pose or badly drawn—In short is it a masterpiece only requiring the little completenesses of foot or finger? Tell us all.... [76]

Alas, Beatrice's response is not recorded. But Whistler could not restrain his enthusiasm over his latest creation when asked by a critic from *The Illustrated London News,* "But tell me, what are you painting over in Paris?" 'Well!' said the painter, 'I am at work on a full-length portrait of a distinguished man, the Comte Robert de Montesquiou. It is a standing figure, and in Paris those who have seen it declare it is quite one of the best things I have ever done.'" [77]

63 *A Selection of Whistler's Painting Equipment,* 1890s, Glasgow, Hunterian Art Gallery

There is no indication of what had become of Bouchor, Whistler's host, but it is apparent from the correspondence that Whistler was still using his studio in the rue Monsieur-le-Prince during March 1892. A letter he sent to Beatrice soon after occupying the space made it clear that it pleased him to the point of wishing to take it over:

> In any case the Studio is such—that we can no longer do without it—and no matter what happens we must own it!…Just fancy an enormous sort of mysterious palatial interior with parqueted floor, and window going up to the roof as who should say—with *every* effect dreamed of—from Rembrant through to the daintiest of pastels! [78]

Nevertheless, having decided to establish a residence in Paris, Whistler had been looking elsewhere in the city for a studio of his own, at one point in mid April visiting a location Montesquiou had spoken of on the Île Saint-Louis. Eventually he located one in Montparnasse at 86 rue Notre-Dame-des-Champs (figs. 53, 67), a street that accommodated more artists' studios than any other in Paris[79] and whose name provoked Whistler to remark, "Only the French have any taste in the naming of streets." [80]

This building contains nine studios. Whistler's was located on the seventh floor (American system), looking south-east over a small court-yard towards the Luxembourg Gardens. It measures 115 square meters.[81] Visitors faced a rugged climb up a spiral staircase of tiny, polished oak steps to reach the artist's aeyrie. Eddy, who posed there in 1894, described the décor ten years later:

79

[Handwritten letter in Whistler's hand]

64 Whistler, *Letter to Beatrice Whistler*
(excerpt), February 1892, Glasgow
University Library

Even the great barn of an attic which was his studio in Paris was
painted by him, so that from its dark—not black—rich oak floor,
along base-boards and walls, to sloping roof, the effect was such
as he sought as an environment for his pictures,—a brown, a
grayish brown, a soft and singular shade of brown, hard to
describe, difficult to see, but delightful to *feel* in its sober and
retiring neutrality....the skylight was well arranged with shades,
so he could keep the light soft and constant; and frequently he
would draw the shades so as to make the room quite dark, and
then view portrait and sitter as they loomed up in shadow.[82]

On May 25, 1892, the artist wrote to Mallarmé of his labor over
this setting: "The studio is coming along nicely—but before showing it to
you I shall need a few more days of perfecting," [83] and to Montesquiou
two months later he added: "We shall emerge from them [packing cases]
to receive you at 86, Rue Notre Dame des Champs...." [84] Whistler kept
this studio until 1901.

While the Whistlers were busily setting up their new Paris
residence at 110 rue du Bac during the summer of 1892, Montesquiou
proposed giving them an Empire bed that had been part of the
furnishings of his apartment in the rue Franklin. The enthusiasm for
Empire furniture shared by Montesquiou and Whistler—and by such
acquaintances of theirs as Beardsley, Boldini, Helleu, La Gandara,
Mallarmé, and Sargent[85]—was enhanced in this case by the distinguished
provenance of this bed: supposedly it had been given to Montesquiou's
great-grandmother, Comtesse Louise-Charlotte de Montesquiou-

Fezensac, by Napoleon himself, in recognition of her services as governess to his son, the King of Rome.[86]

Coming from such an august source, this early nineteenth-century bed (fig. 65) is a surprisingly modest production. Unidentified by any maker's mark, its boat-shaped mahogany carcass is ornamented on one side with gilt-bronze mounts in the form of laurel ropes terminating at the center in swans that flank a lyre. At the apexes of the sides are swan heads with curved necks in solid gilt bronze. The pattern of symmetrical laurel is strikingly similar to the ornamentation over the portal of the house in which Montesquiou was born—the Hôtel de Béthune, 60 rue de Varenne (fig. 22)—and over the windows of that built by his father around 1863 at 41 quai d'Orsay (fig. 23), where he spent his youth. In both these instances, laurel branches frame the initial M. After Whistler's death, the bed eventually ended up at the Victoria and Albert Museum, presented in 1933 by Rosalind Birnie Philip, to whom Whistler had given it in 1896, after the death of his wife.

The Whistlers reacted enthusiastically to Montesquiou's gift, the artist writing from his studio with tantalizing ambiguity in August or late September:

> We are enchanted—as our missive [probably a telegram] said— and as you had surely guessed before receiving it—You produce surprises like Aladin and rightly so—and the splendid boatbed that could only have come from your magic lamp equals and goes far beyond all the hopes that could have aroused in us either the envy of friendship, or the unbridled patience, even of Collectors like ourselves! I was going to say too that I recognize as well the lovely vengeance of the Poet for the "sixty sessions"—that I never doubted—and which are now inscribed, for ever and ever, in my file—but this moment of joy is scarcely that of regret—and we want to think only of the superb present that our charming friend has sent us!…For the rest—you tell me many gracious and friendly things in your letter—and as to your part—that is perfect—As for mine—and just as you put it, "sixty sessions" is a lot, but not enough!! and so my dear friend, until our next coming together. Mistress Beatrix, who has been ill of late, or her letter would have accompanied mine, asks me to convey a thousand choice messages while awaiting that she write you "her impressions" herself! [87]

In due time, Beatrice's letter was sent, in English, as her French was not equal to her husband's:

> I cannot tell you how pleased I am with the wonderful bed—! and how difficult it is for me to thank you enough for it—! It is so beautiful that the room in which it is going to be placed, will really—I believe—have to be begun all over again—to make it at all worthy of it. Since the day I first saw it at your home, it has been my dreame, to some day find one something like it, and I have seen several—but nothing to equal it, and I, at last, made up my mind that I should have to wait a long time before I found it, and now—it has come! straight from fairyland! [88]

Montesquiou acknowledged this note, addressing its writer as "the beautiful Saskhia [wife of Rembrandt], the brilliant Hélène

Fourment [wife of Rubens]." [89] He acknowledged Whistler's as well, but his response survives only in fragments, a condition that adds to the obscurity of its meaning: "It now remains for me to know whether I should give an order to *set sail* (for this boat-bed) to the rue Notre-Dame des Champs…or rather await the final blossoming of the *mysteries* to install the epithalamium of the boat-bed in its final setting…more appropriate to its condition than the studio." He went on to make reference to "the arrangement in rose and grey…the grey lord," by which he may have been alluding to the other version of his portrait, and concluded with a rather challenging remark about the possibility of future posing sessions: "Furthermore if you wish to work a little again and on a small scale on my *irremovability as a Whistlerian model,* I have a *petition* to present to you from a *very great man* (who is only me) on *this very subject.*" [90]

Certain phrases in Whistler's letter cited above could be interpreted as suggesting that Montesquiou was intending the bed to be his payment for the portrait and that Whistler was accepting this proposal, notably "the lovely vengeance of the Poet for the 'sixty sessions'" and "as to your part—that is perfect." In 1968, I suggested this interpretation of the gift, inasmuch as no other record of payment seemed to exist,[91] and none has come to light since then. As Antoine Bertrand has demonstrated in his account of Montesquiou's reducing to near-bankruptcy the Abbaye de Créteil, an idealistic union of printers and artists,[92] the poet was accustomed to extracting from artists and tradesmen, at no cost to himself, valuable works of art and luxury goods. The point was emphasized by a close friend of Montesquiou, Élisabeth de Clermont-Tonnerre, who recalled: "The most celebrated artists of Paris worked for him: Meunier bound his books, which Madeleine Lemaire and Besnard illustrated; Gallé and Lalique offered him gifts of glass, the perfumer Georges Klotz, perfumes; famous greenhouses sent him their flowers and fruits; ladies lent him their automobiles; musicians played for him; sopranos sang without fee.…" [93] Yet occasionally an artist such as Besnard would refuse to execute a portrait etching without reward, and Rodin declined to reduce the price of a bust Montesquiou thought of commissioning from him. In view of all this, it is not inconceivable that Montesquiou sought to satisfy the financial expectations of Whistler, a passionate collector of Empire furniture, with a bed whose provenance went directly back to the Emperor himself.

The prices Whistler expected for a portrait varied widely in the 1890s, the sums often adjusted to the sitters' means. As Eddy recalled: "When Whistler did part with a picture he had no faculty for getting a high price. His prices were very uncertain. To one person he might ask a round sum, to another small,—just as the mood seized him, the price having no particular relation to the painting." [94] The Parisian journalist Saint-Charles, writing in November 1891, stated, "The University of Edinburgh paid him 35,000 francs for the portrait of Carlyle and, ever since, Whistler sells his paintings for 35,000 francs or doesn't charge for them at all." [95] It was in fact The Corporation of Glasgow that bought the portrait of Carlyle in April 1891 for 1,000 guineas (about 25,000 francs), a hefty price; but eight months later Whistler accepted 4,000 francs in order to have the portrait of his mother enter the collections of the Luxembourg Museum (and eventually the Louvre). In 1892 the artist was quoted as asking 500 or 525 guineas to paint the head of Lady Eden; a year later John James Cowan was quoted 600 guineas for a half-length portrait or small full-length, 400 guineas for a head; Arthur Eddy paid 350 guineas for his large full-length (fig. 59) in 1894; the early Sarasate portrait (fig. 124) was sold to Carnegie Institute in 1896 for £ 900 (a year earlier £ 2,000 had been asked for it); in 1897 George W. Vanderbilt paid 2,000 guineas for his full-length; and half-lengths of Canfield (fig. 74) and of Freer cost £ 500 in 1901 and 1902 respectively.[96] According to financial experts, £ 1 in 1892 was equivalent in value to 25 francs then and £ 55 today; 1 franc in 1892 is equivalent in value to 18 francs today.[97] Confirming this, Edmond de Goncourt recorded an instance of Whistler speaking on the subject of prices, when he noted on May 15, 1891:

> At the *Grenier,* Tissot repeated today a conversation of Whistler's that he heard in London: "Millais does portraits for which he is paid 3000 pounds—75,000 francs—for my part, I want to achieve earning as much as he in doing them for 1000 pounds. But since I must do three instead of one.…" [98]

In 1895, a year after Montesquiou had taken firm possession of his portrait, he was quoted, when asked what must one pay for a portrait by Whistler, as replying, "One must pay him more than one can." [99] But Whistler, in his furious note to Montesquiou after the latter had sold the portrait to Canfield in 1902, said the poet had acquired the painting "for a song." [100]

Whatever the significance of the Empire bed, the installation of the Whistlers' apartment had advanced sufficiently by October 1892 for the artist to request delivery of it: "As for the new 'little Chelsea'—there are a thousand things to perfect before the opening—but the 'beautiful Empire boat' remains always a consolation and a hope!—Can we send someone to get it? Or do you wish to get it under full sail, and navigate it to the new harbor—Rue du Bac-No. 110!!!" [101] An undated letter from Whistler to Montesquiou suggested that the artist was present when the bed was removed from the rue Franklin: "I hope that everything went well this morning? I was present at the departure, and everything was in perfect condition." [102]

The next year—1893—saw several developments: the presentation to the Whistlers of the second edition of *Les Chauves-Souris,* provoking some annoyance on the artist's part over the choice of illustration for the bat image; the publication of a new volume of poetry, *Le Chef des odeurs suaves,* that included *White Rose* dedicated to Whistler; various social invitations; and Montesquiou's pathetic request (in English) to Beatrice that she get her husband back at work on the portrait, pleading "…I claim your powerfull and gracious assistance upon your cruel and marvellous husband for see at last flutter around the mysterious master-piece the slow butterfly!" [103]

In fact the portrait was now suffering the fate of many another recently completed work by Whistler: it was languishing in the studio of the master who could not bear to give it up. Eddy, who had managed to get his portrait painted and delivered in one year, described the usual practice of the artist:

> Whistler was seldom so satisfied with a portrait that he was willing to part with it. He could always see things he wished to

change,—partly no doubt, because his impression of his subject changed from day to day,—and he would often keep a portrait by him for months and years before exhibiting. In fact he exhibited a like reserve about nearly all his work....Childless, his paintings were his children, and to part with one was like the parting of mother and child.[104]

Then suddenly Whistler agreed to release the portrait for showing at the 1894 Salon exhibition of the Société Nationale des Beaux-Arts, sending Montesquiou this curiously apologetic telegram:

How right you were, dear Poet!—and how mad I was!!!—It is *splendid* the real Dartagnan!—and the false one has disappeared before its entrance in a thousand pieces! I shall never pardon myself for my unworthy modesty and fear—but you will try to forget it before your beautiful picture, no? I could never thank you enough for all your friendly and kindly actions—and I shall be ashamed for the hardships and inconveniences that those useless sessions caused you—But what an inspiration to have sent for it! and *just* in time—for an ultimatum came from the Champ de Mars [site of the exhibition]—demanding *immediately* all the canvases. *So, it is gone*—the Black Knight!—with the others— except for the poor Pink Tulip—who has not finished her toilette [*Rose et or: La Tulipe*].[105]

Besides explaining the fate of *Impressions de gris perle* (see p. 66), this crucial document effectively concludes the history of Montesquiou's portrait up to its presentation to the public on April 25, 1894.

65 French, *Bedstead,* mahogany and gilt
bronze, early nineteenth-century,
London, Victoria and Albert Museum,
provenance Napoleon I, Montesquiou,
Whistler

The Salon of 1894, and Beyond

On Monday, April 25, 1894, the Parisian public was finally permitted to view Whistler's portrait of Robert de Montesquiou, the work so long veiled by its subject in secrecy. Packed once again in its crate, the tall canvas (233 x 160 cm. in the frame) had been lowered through the window of the artist's studio (fig. 67) with a pulley,[1] and delivered in mid March to the building south of the Eiffel Tower on the Champ-de-Mars that was the setting for the annual exhibition of the Société Nationale des Beaux-Arts.

This organization had been founded only four years earlier, under the leadership of Meissonier, in reaction against the more conservative, state-endorsed Société des Artistes Français, whose exhibitions took place in the Palais de l'Industrie across the Seine on the Champs-Élysées. A third Salon exhibiting simultaneously with the others was that of the Indépendants; featuring the Neo-Impressionists, its exhibitions were held in the Jardins des Tuileries. Writing in 1890, Ernest Hoschedé predicted that the Salon of the Champ-de-Mars would be the public's favorite among the three, for it "will shelter at once those who respect the traditions of great art, the pioneers of new formulae, and the audacious ones of genius....It will be the Salon of art for art's sake." [2]

In 1894, Whistler chose to exhibit there fourteen works—seven paintings and seven lithographs. Among the paintings were three seascapes and three portraits, the former group comprising *Violet and Silver: A Deep Sea* (Art Institute of Chicago), *Dark Blue and Silver* (Hill-Stead Museum, Farmington, Connecticut), and *Violet and Blue: Among the Rollers* (present whereabouts unknown), and the latter group portraits of Montesquiou (No. 1186, *Noir et or:—Portrait du comte Robert de Montesquiou-Fezensac*), Mrs. Walter Sickert (Fogg Art Museum, Cambridge, Massachusetts), and the soon-to-be-controversial likeness of Lady Eden (Hunterian Museum and Art Gallery, Glasgow). Though *Rose et or: La Tulipe* (also in the Hunterian Museum) was listed in the catalogue, as No. 1184, Whistler thought it too unfinished to exhibit. The lithographs included several views of the Luxembourg Gardens and a portrait of Mallarmé. In terms of installation, an unsigned article in the *Art Journal* of 1894 noted that "the Champ de Mars Salon reserves its chief centre for [Whistler's] canvases." [3]

Open to artists from all nations who were willing to subject their entries to a French jury, the Salon of the Société Nationale des Beaux-Arts of 1894 attracted a bewildering range of talents responsible for the 2,215 works shown. They included Béraud, Besnard (see fig. 42), Blanche, Boutet de Monvel, Carolus-Duran, Carrière, Cazin, Dagnan-Bouveret, Gervex, Helleu, Le Sidaner, Puvis de Chavannes (president of the Société that year), Sisley, Tissot, and Suzanne Valadon. Among the non-French representatives there were, besides Whistler, Conder, La Gandara, Charles Dana Gibson, Hawkins, Hodler, Lavery (fig. 69), Liebermann, Melchers, Sargent, Winnaretta Singer (the American heiress recently married to the Prince de Polignac), Stevens (see fig. 109), and Thaulow. Almost last, but certainly not least, in the section devoted to *Objets d'art* there appeared, as No. 465, a *Psyché de glycines* (present whereabouts unknown) whose composition, preparatory drawings, and wax models were the work of Montesquiou; its marquetry was executed by Émile Gallé, who exhibited

66 Unknown photographer, *Photograph of Whistler's Portrait of Montesquiou,* before 1902, Paris, private collection, provenance Montesquiou

67 F. Morellec, *Exterior of 86 rue Notre-Dame-des-Champs,* photographed in 1994, Whistler's studio at top center with arched window

as well a phial engraved with a line of Montesquiou's poetry: "*La bonté de la nuit caresse l'âme sombre.*"

Edmond de Goncourt attended the private opening of the Salon on April 24 and recorded his impressions in his diary that day, noting:

> I meet Raffaelli, Rosny on Guillaume's arm, Helleu, Blanche, La Gandara, Montesquiou-Fezensac, who takes me over to see his portrait by Whistler, a portrait in which I find a marvelous rendition of the clothing, but a very inferior execution of the badly drawn figure, of the depressing flesh tones, dirty, messy.[4]

Also among the opening-day crowd appeared Camille Pissarro, who wrote one of the first commentaries on Whistler's portrait of Montesquiou—in a letter to his son Lucien dated Thursday, April 28:

> Before writing to you, I wanted to have visited the different exhibitions in order to give you a report. I went to the Champ de Mars on opening day and again yesterday, as well as to the Indépendants.…As in other years, nothing extraordinary at the Champ de Mars beyond Whistler and Puvis de Chavannes.
>
> The *Portrait of Montesquiou* by Whistler is an extremely beautiful thing, for gesture, refined elegance, and of a very great unity, obtained, it is true, by tricks, in the manner of Velázquez, rather than really painted.[5]

Another artist who was quick to spot Montesquiou's portrait at the exhibition was John Singer Sargent, over from London. Graham Robertson, whom Sargent was painting at the time (fig. 68), recorded the artist's reaction to Montesquiou's portrait:

> After [my] picture was well advanced it was laid by for a short time while the artist took a holiday in Paris, and when I started sittings again I found him much perturbed. "I say," he began, "did you ever see Whistler's portrait of Comte Robert de Montesquiou?" "No," said I. "They never would let me see it while it was being painted. Why?" "Well, I'd never seen it either," said Sargent, "until I came across it just now in the Champs de Mars. It's just like this! Everybody will say that I've copied it."… And in truth a few people did make the remark, though there was really but little resemblance. Both canvases showed a tall, thin figure in black against a dark background, but the likeness ceased there and, as a picture, the Sargent was by far the finer. The Whistler was not of his best—the blacks were black, not the lovely vaporous dimness of the "Rosa Corder"; the portrait was quite worthy neither of the painter nor the model, for the delicate moulding of Robert de Montesquiou's features was hardly suggested; but Whistler was not then quite equal to the physical exertion of dealing with so large a canvas…it was the last large picture that he ever completed [*sic*]. The Sargent, on the other hand, was of the artist's best period and he was painting something that he had "seen" pictorially and for some unknown reason had wished to perpetuate.[6]

Writing to a friend over forty years later, Graham Robertson returned to the subject:

> Thank you for telling me about the Frick Whistlers. So two of my shots were right—Montesquiou and the Leyland picture.

Rosa Corder (fig. 123) and the pink Lady Meux are first-raters, Rosa almost his best picture. The Leyland is so-so, and the Montesquiou not really good. It gives no idea of Robert's beauty of feature or dignity of bearing, and as a picture it's not up to the Whistler standard. Though I wouldn't as a rule dream of comparing the painters, I think that Sargent's "Me" is the better picture. Sargent was accused of copying the Montesquiou, but he didn't. My portrait was nearly finished before he saw the Whistler.…I only saw the Montesquiou portrait once and was bitterly disappointed with it.…The head is nothing.…And the pose is limp, weak, "gone at the knees," giving no hint of Robert's nervous alertness. Robert was beautiful—a strange epithet to apply to a man but I can think of no other word for his clear-cut perfection of feature and his grace of body. He was very slender, almost fragile-looking, but not in the least floppy. He was not strong and he told me himself that the weight of the heavy fur coat over his arm tired him very much when he was posing for Whistler, but he could never have looked the squiggly little worm shown in the picture. I enclose an old photograph of him which may give you an idea of the face. It is not a face to forget, is it?… Whistler was too old when he painted the Montesquiou. He should not have attempted a picture on that scale.[7]

Yet another artist who would have studied Montesquiou's portrait with particular interest was John Lavery (1856–1941), who was exhibiting at the same Salon, under No. 693, his *Portrait de R. B. Cunninghame Graham* (fig. 69), which rather resembled Whistler's work. The debt that both artists owed to Velázquez' precedent was acknowledged by Lavery, who said that he had painted the extravagant Cunninghame Graham "frankly in the manner of Velasquez, full-length and life size, a harmony in brown." [8] Even more than echoing the pose of Whistler's portrait, which Lavery could have seen during visits to the artist's Paris studio in 1892 and 1893, the Irish artist intentionally sought, like Whistler, to project the special mystique of his subject, recalling: "I think I did something to help Graham in the creation of his masterpiece—himself." [9] No less a personage than George Bernard Shaw felt that Lavery had succeeded in both his aims: "He [Cunninghame Graham] is, I understand, a Spanish hidalgo, hence the superbity of his portrait by Lavery (Velasquez being no longer available)." [10]

The Studio reported on May 1 that "Monsieur de Montesquiou, correctly white-gloved and befrocked in grey, was to be seen [at the Salon] almost every day, open to the ox-gaze of the browsing public." [11] Montesquiou must also have subscribed to a news-clipping service to keep a record of the critical reactions to his portrait, for seven pages in Vol. CCLXXVII of his papers preserved at the Bibliothèque Nationale de France are devoted to these columns, carefully pasted down and identified by a meticulous secretary. Some excerpts are quoted below to suggest their range of opinion—from describing the portrait as "a pure abomination" to calling it "a symphony of all that is great in art." [12] Occasionally the reviews encourage us to look at the portrait more closely.

68 J. S. Sargent, *Portrait of W. Graham Robertson,* oil, 1894, London, Tate Gallery

On the contentious side, the most serious article was that of Roger Milès, published in *Le Salon de 1894*. Springing to the attack, the critic wrote:

> M. James Whistler has a lot of talent and he knows it, but M. James Whistler…wouldn't be saddened to make us believe that he has more talent than he really does. After imposing on himself the strangeness of his manner, he might have come back not to another vision—he knows how, by the way, to modify the latter—but to another form of presentation. For several years now, to remind us that he pretends to be a colorist, everything he paints bears a title that greatly resembles those inscribed on the drawers of ribbon and silk merchants; he catalogues: *Violet and Silver; Blue and Violet; Pink and Red; Red and Violet; Black and Gold; Brown and Gold*, etc., and since, no doubt, he fears that the indication might be insufficient to guide the visitor, he adds a more explicit title:…*Portrait of M. le Comte X., Portrait of Lady Y.* For many, who allow themselves to be easily taken in by such flummery, there is in all this an artistic striving of an inspired intensity.…For others, who judge things more soberly, there is in all this a lack of simplicity, a constant need to stand out from one's contemporaries.…I appreciate infinitely the talent of M. Whistler.…Only it is time that he let his works alone glorify his name, instead of participating himself, with an ease totally lacking in modesty, in glorifying his works.[13]

Patriotic suspicion of the foreigner registered itself: "The portrait of *M. Robert de Montesquiou* is no doubt also called a masterpiece?…I am almost ashamed of being French to such a point that I cannot understand and appreciate these marvels of an art foreign to our national temperament." [14] So did the incomprehension of the Philistines who dogged Whistler's early days: "We presume the 'advanced' school of critics will tell us that Mr. Whistler's portrait of the Comte de Montesquiou-Fezensac is the portrait of the year. We can only see a figure about ten heads high, with a colourless pasty face, which nothing but absolute infatuation could accept as a fine picture." [15]

However, on April 24—the day before the public opening—an unidentified critic would write in *Paris:*

> The portrait of M. de Montesquiou is a work of superb style, of great elegance. From the feet to the head, it is a strong and refined effigy. And yet, what's there? Only a young man of our own time, captured with subtlety, but simply, and standing tall, one hand elegantly resting on a thin cane. But the attitude is so right, so at ease, the head is so finely studied, then so temperately indicated in its essential features, the entire movement is so lively, and the harmony, pure black with some relief in grey, is so sonorous and so profound that—all of a sudden—you have a work that is significant, lasting, and the proof of a master.[16]

One of several critics to find a mediumistic quality in the portrait wrote in *Le XIXème Siècle:*

> One's attention always comes back to this apparition that seems to escape from the shadows and advance toward you. M. de Montesquiou is standing, in dress clothes, his overcoat [*sic*]

69 Sir J. Lavery, *Portrait of R. B. Cunninghame Graham,* oil, 1894, Glasgow Art Gallery and Museum

carelessly thrown over his arm; his princely stature is silhouetted in the darkness with a supreme elegance; apart from the facial mask marked with a strong will and illuminated with a penetrating and gentle look, apart from the white areas of the shirt and glove, there are nothing but shadows, and the impeccable control of M. Whistler has triumphed in the notation of all these blacks, one lifted over the other. However, more than by the execution, one is conquered by the violent seizure of character. Since Velázquez, we cannot recall the male portrait comprehended in this way, with such fullness. I don't know whether M. le comte de Montesquiou is completely happy with the portrait M. Whistler has made of him, but, in any case, the severity of this esthete who poses and struts has been fully, completely captured.[17]

An unsigned article in *The Nineteenth Century* predicted the future of Whistler's portrait with eery precision:

His portrait of Comte Robert de Montesquiou has neither weakness nor limitation. It is a complete, an absolute work of art, that is all. The figure is posed with a distinction that could scarcely be surpassed. The point of the foot, the turn of the wrist, the hand which holds a cane like a sword, the head thrown back in an attitude of insolence—these are arranged and painted by a master. The simplicity which dominates the portrait is as remarkable as the mystery enshrouding this harmony in black and silver [*sic*]. The artist, as is his wont, has made no more of his materials than the exposition demands, and the result is a portrait that might have strayed from some noble gallery which is its inevitable destiny....Before all it is obvious that Mr. Whistler arrives at his goal without eccentricity and without an outrage upon the traditions of art. He is a link in the long, unbroken chain of the masters. In his art there is neither uncertainty nor experiment.[18]

The noted critic Gustave Geffroy, writing in *La Justice,* also described the portrait as "a work that feels as though it belongs in a museum." He went on to say:

This portrait of Monsieur de Montesquiou will one day be regarded as a history painting, that is certain....The man, thin and forceful...advances from the shadows, and rises up like a darkened statue on the softly luminous floor. The mixture of light and shadow envelops the silhouette, illuminates the dress coat, veils the whiteness of the glove and shirt front, the warm tones of the flesh, leaving sharp only the drawing of the hand, the position of the thumb, the curve of the shoulder, the definition of the mouth, the focus of the gaze. It is a unique mixture, delicately measured out, of bravado and refinement, of irony and melancholy. Moreover, this portrait possesses what all beautiful portraits do. It contains a quantity of enigmas that will leave viewers dreaming constantly. Who is this passer-by? where is he going? what is he thinking about? When a picture asks you these questions, pursues you, obsesses you by the silent reality it affirms and the mystery it harbors, you can predict its power with certainty, the prolongation of its destiny.[19]

The initial fears of Montesquiou and the Comtesse Greffulhe that

No. 1186.

70 Unknown artist, *Caricature of Whistler's Portrait of Montesquiou*, from *Punch*, May 26, 1894, New York Public Library

Whistler's portrait might give the impression only of a "chic young man from the end of the nineteenth century" seem largely to have been unwarranted, though the critic of *Le Temps* did observe, "The poet of *Les Chauves-Souris* is right there, just as we know him, just as one could easily imagine him without knowing him…deliciously snob." [20] Another wrote, "It's Monsieur de Montesquiou-Fezensac, a tall, stiff gentleman in the dark, but very chic." [21]

The period's delight in caricatures of susceptible works in the Salon was satisfied by at least two in 1894—*Punch's* rendition of Whistler's "funny figure" (fig. 70), which appeared on May 26, and Albert Guillaume's colored image of the portrait (fig. 71) labelled "*Le Hareng saur*" ("The Smoked Herring"). Montesquiou's secretary identified this as coming from *Le Figaro illustré*, but in fact it appeared in another, unidentified journal.[22]

The final days of the Salon exhibition must have been affected by the assassination of the president of the French Republic, Sadi Carnot, on June 24, the gravest of a series of anarchists' acts that had troubled Paris in recent months. By early July, Whistler's portrait had been transported to Montesquiou's new residence in the town of Versailles—93 avenue de Paris—the first house on the town side of the old toll-house, about a half-mile away from the palace, down a broad, shaded road that had been laid out in the late seventeenth century. The "Pavillon Montesquiou," as the poet called his new abode (fig. 72), was a small building with several wings, the oldest of which dated back to 1683, when the site was just a small farm. According to Montesquiou's notes, the property belonged to the following succession of owners: in 1768, to a Monsieur Defeutre, butler to Marie-Antoinette when she was Dauphine; in 1778, to a Monsieur Cazier de Rennouville, equerry to Louis XV's daughter, Madame Adélaïde; in 1785, to the Baron de Méré, a naval captain; in 1788, to a Monsieur Sanson, sword-bearer to Louis XVI; in 1821, to a Monsieur Porta, a banker; and in 1827, to the Vicomte d'Alsace.[23] The house still stands today.

The inauguration of the pavilion was to have taken place on May 24, but it was postponed until the 30th because of bad weather. The event, called an "Impromptu de Versailles," featured Sarah Bernhardt reciting André Chénier's "Ode à Versailles," combined with musical performances, followed by a sumptuous buffet. The press coverage was extensive (see fig. 43), most articles beginning with a description of Montesquiou's muse, such as: "It is…the Comtesse Greffulhe, much admired, who covers a light-colored dress embroidered with hydrangeas— the preferred flower of the master of the house—beneath the vaporous pleats of a coat of mauve chiffon." [24] If Whistler attended, his presence was not noted. Proust, however, was there and described the event in his article entitled "Fête littéraire à Versailles," published in *Le Gaulois* on May 31.

On August 1, 1894, *La Revue illustrée* published an extensively illustrated article devoted to the poet's new residence—"Une Heure chez le Comte Robert de Montesquiou"—that opens with telling references to the portrait:

> M. de Montesquiou is now in the prime of life and one has only to look at his so evocative portrait by Whistler to understand that

he brings to life all the presumptions of his class and all the desire not to be mixed up with the masses, the odious unifier of all feelings. And yet, since, no matter what, we must resemble one another: M. de Montesquiou, albeit wearing the exterior clothing of our time, the suit that resembles yours, the collar that resembles the one of a minister of M. Casimir-Périer [president of the Republic], is reduced to distinguishing himself from you, from us, by details. It is the grey glove which, in Whistler's portrait, recalls the nobles at the Spanish court (cf. fig. 128), it is the malacca cane thrust out in front, as provocative as a gentleman's sword ready to be drawn for a duel if necessary; it is the eye above all, piercing, sharp, and yet which rests only lightly on men and things, as if it found it useless to look too long, as if it knew that nothing deserves the effort of being studied deeply.[25]

Though the article provides five photographic views of the interior of this "home *délicieux*," furnished alternately in Japanese (see fig. 25) and Empire style, Whistler's portrait appears in none, perhaps because it was still on view at the Salon when the photographs were taken. It was, however, given a full-page reproduction.

Despite his deep attachment to Versailles (see fig. 42), in 1896 Montesquiou moved back to the Left Bank in Paris, living first at 80 rue de l'Université for two years, then moving to 14 avenue Bosquet, where he remained through 1900. No records have survived showing the installation of these residences, but still attached to the portrait's stretcher is a shipping label from the Chemins de Fer de l'Ouest recording its transfer from Versailles (Gare Rive Gauche) to Paris (Gare de Montparnasse). In later years, the poet would maintain a secondary residence at Versailles, 5 rue La Fayette.

Montesquiou's next abode—at 96 boulevard Maillot in Neuilly—was soon publicized by the poet himself in *La Revue contemporaine,* with an article announcing the sonorous name of this dwelling: "Le Pavillon des Muses." In a view of the dining room (fig. 73), Whistler's portrait appears, standing on the floor alongside a monumental stone fireplace blithely attributed to Puget. The article made specific reference to it: "Another portrait, by Whistler, that of the master of this house, a masterpiece, a celebrated canvas: a symphony in black major, illuminated with a few creamy whites of the linen, of the pearly grey chinchilla, and of the glove, gilded with the amber tones of the face." [26] Émile Berr, describing the June 20 inauguration of the Pavillon des Muses in *Le Figaro,* also made reference to the portrait "in the dining room nearby, where Whistler and Helleu triumph, with exquisite portraits." [27] Writing about Montesquiou's American tour for the *Paris World* in 1903, a correspondent recalled the portrait's presence in the dining room of the Pavillon des Muses and its lifelike character:

> To the right of the majestic mantelpiece, there stands against a screen or support a noble picture by Whistler—the portrait of the master of the house himself. A noted canvas this....Monsieur de Montesquiou regards this portrait of himself as a masterpiece.... I turned again and saw him, a tall, dark figure against a darker background, in the deepening shadows of the waning winter's day. And as he waved his hand, in token of farewell, I thought of

those sombre but impressive pictures of Velasquez in their rich deep tones and subtle shades.[28]

The Pavillon des Muses—perhaps the most celebrated of Montesquiou's residences—was demolished to make way for an apartment house, designed in the rich art déco style of Rubio de Teran, dated 1935.

After the exhibition of 1894 and Montesquiou's taking possession of his portrait, contacts with Whistler were rare. New Year's greetings were sent by the poet from Azay-le-Rideau on December 31, 1894,[29] and reiterated a few days later, when Montesquiou, announcing his intention to reside again in Paris, lamented Whistler's absence from the capital:

> In vain I took the route toward the mysterious garden [Whistler's, at 110 rue du Bac], now closed, silent, and deserted, at the very moment when a new residence in Paris seemed to favor me with a precious neighborly intercourse....The memory of you is constantly present, as is all that is beautiful and noble, spiritual, and gallant throughout our vicissitudes, and above them. I hasten to send you my best wishes. Receive them as from one of those who admires you the most and loves you with the most affectionate respect.[30]

At this time, Whistler was preoccupied with his wife's declining health, and then, in early 1895, with the preparations for her sister's marriage in Paris to Charles Whibley. Beatrice would die of cancer early the year after that—on May 10, 1896. Montesquiou soon afterwards wrote the artist:

> I shared with you the beautiful affection that made you happy. I followed you through the uncertainties that it called up in you. I walk with you now in the sorrow that her loss brings to you. And it is from my heart, as you well know, sincerely moved and profoundly respectful of your great merit, confronting such a painful challenge, that I address to you, you and yours...my truest condolences and my most ardent sympathy. Think of me, my dear Friend, at the time of a possible reunion, and believe in my most devoted feelings.[31]

That Whistler never responded to this letter disturbed Montesquiou, but the artist was wrapped up in troubles over the next few years. On December 4, 1898, the poet addressed this penultimate letter to his old friend, accompanied by copies of his recently published *Les Roseaux pensants* (1897) and *Les Autels privilégiés* (1898):

> Here are two little books, which (still without daring to approach so precious a subject *directly*) occasionally speaking of you to others, would really like once to speak to you. I should also strongly fear that my silence, even subject to yours, would risk creating and maintaining a misunderstanding, which, with you, would be cruel. I have written to you several times since your great sorrow, without ever receiving a reply; and I did not believe that I had to insist with respect to this natural form of true grief, that is silence. I know too well the content of your words, not to respect your silence. Still, in faithful and glorious memory, I make a point of telling you again from time to time, that today, like yesterday and tomorrow, my own silence, like my own words,

71 A. Guillaume, *Whistler, Le Hareng saur* ("The Smoked Herring"), unidentified Paris journal, May 1894, Paris, Bibliothèque Nationale de France

will always contain for you the most admiring attachment, My dear Master, and my dear Friend.[32]

Four years of silence followed, to be broken with the startling news that Montesquiou had sold his portrait by Whistler to Richard A. Canfield (1855–1914), once the manager of the world's greatest private gambling operation, in New York, and a close friend of Whistler's.

Canfield (fig. 74) was yet another extraordinary figure to participate in the saga of Whistler's portrait. Born in New Bedford, Massachusetts, of distinguished stock, he was educated only through grammar school, then had a number of minor jobs until he discovered his skill and luck at gambling. His winnings enabled him to make a first trip to Europe in 1876. In 1885 he was sentenced to prison for six months for operating a gambling house, a period he later pronounced the happiest in his life because he had acquired there, through reading, an enthusism for art. He opened a gambling club in New York in 1887, another at Saratoga Springs in 1893, and one in Newport in 1897.

Canfield commissioned his portrait from Whistler in 1901 and started to pose in London in March 1902, continuing the following year from January through May. Even though he claimed to have posed every day, the two men apparently spent so much time conversing that the painting never was completed. Whistler dubbed the portrait "His Reverence," probably because its suggestion of clerical garb gave a deceptive air of respectability to the subject. Just after Whistler's death, Canfield told a reporter for the *New York Sun* of the artist's last words to him as he was about to embark for America in mid May of 1903:

> You are going home tomorrow, to my home as well as yours, and you won't be coming back until autumn. I've just been thinking that maybe you'd better take the picture with you. "His Reverence" will do very well as he is, and maybe there won't be any work in me when you come back. I believe I would rather think of you as having this clerical gentleman in your collection, for I've a notion it's the best work I've done.[33]

Canfield instead gambled on returning to London once more to have his portrait completed, but Whistler died on July 17, and his legatee, Rosalind Birnie Philip, sent "His Reverence" from the artist's studio to the London dealer W. Marchant for delivery to Canfield.

It was Canfield, during the period of his posing for the artist, who informed Whistler of purchasing the Montesquiou portrait, with this letter from Paris, dated October 22, 1902: "You will be surprised and I hope pleased to learn that I have bought from Count Robert de Montesquiou, his portrait by yourself. It is still in Paris in my agent's hands, where I ordered it to be kept, hoping that you might send for me to return, and I did not want to miss seeing it, by passing it on the ocean." [34] Whistler, apparently devastated by the news, replied soon after: "Cable detailed story Montesquiou purchase. What refusals, what sum irresistibly accepted?" [35] Canfield supplied the basic information:

> The facts in the Montesquiou portrait purchase as written to me by Monsieur Arnold Seligmann are these: I had requested him to try to buy the portrait, and had told him I would give 75,000 f. and his commission. After some slight delay, Seligmann cabled me that he had bought it. In a few days his letter came, in which

he said he had paid le comte 60,000 f. and I forwarded draft for same plus commission. His next note enclosed Montesquiou's receipt and his own. At once I cabled him to keep the portrait until my arrival, and to keep my name as buyer a secret.[36]

In a cable dated December 17, 1902, Canfield specified what commission Arnold Seligmann (fig. 75) had received for handling the sale: "Seligman [*sic*] paid Montesquiou 60,000 francs. I paid him commission 10%."[37] Another cable of the same date informed Whistler, "Seligman wrote me that Montesquiou refused 50,000 francs last year therefore he offered 60."[38] After these transactions, the portrait was sent to Whistler's studio in London.

Whistler, who frequently had had the disheartening experience of seeing works of his purchased for a pittance later sold for extravagant prices, was particularly outraged to have an avowed friend do this. He fired off a letter to Montesquiou, of which only two rough drafts have survived, now among the Whistler papers in Glasgow: "Bravo Montesquiou!—both the beautiful words and the bequest to the Louvre have had to yield to American dollars—'By necessity the nobly born must nobly do!'—and the portrait acquired as a Poet, for a song, is sold again as the Jew of the rue Lafitte, for ten times that song!—Congratulations!"[39]

This is the only one of Whistler's letters that Montesquiou did not preserve. Considering the man, his response to it was remarkably restrained:

> Monsieur Whistler, The abusive letter that I have just received from you, and whose terms I should not accept from any other person, encounters, all the same, in my memories, feelings that have never wavered, and never shall waver, in regard to your Art, and to your Person. Certainly, I should have wished to consult you, and I tried to do so; but you were away; and several mailings of books and of letters, that remained without response, for years, without anything, on my part, that would have motivated this indifference, made me believe that you had forgotten me. It was then that I believed I could make a decision that seemed to guarantee worthily the future of a very noble work of art, at the same time showing the respect due your great fame. Robert de Montesquiou.[40]

Before he gave up his portrait, the poet had it photographed and set the print in a Whistlerian gilded frame (fig. 66).

Whistler's official biographers Elizabeth and Joseph Pennell were at hand to witness and record the artist's reaction to the news of the sale of the Montesquiou portrait:

> [We] went to Whistler's and found him looking again most frightfully ill. He was excited over the fact that Montesquiou had sold his portrait—"Montesquiou, the descendant of a long distinguished line of French noblemen. I painted it for a mere nothing—*mon cher,* you understand, Montesquiou said, and it was arranged between gentlemen. And now Montesquiou has sold it, no doubt for a large sum of money! He had written to me, but his letter is feeble—he had not heard from me for so long, thought I had forgotten him—no excuse at all."[41]

72 Unknown photographer, *The Pavillon Montesquiou, Versailles,* from *La Revue illustrée,* August 1, 1894, Washington, Library of Congress, Yturri at left, Montesquiou at right

Within the raw fury of the missive Whistler had sent Montesquiou may lie, among other things, the answer to the question of what the latter paid for his portrait. If it was in fact one-tenth of the 60,000 francs Whistler knew the poet had received from Canfield—namely 6,000 francs, or its equivalent value as an Empire bed—then the amount would have been only half again the bargain price at which the artist had sold the portrait of his mother to the French government in 1891. As for the anti-Semitic jibe in the note, it is worth recalling that this was expressed while the Dreyfus case was being heatedly debated, and that it was in line with Whistler's familiar disparagement of American blacks, as well as his totally unsympathetic attitude toward Oscar Wilde after the latter's release from prison. That Whistler's insult reflects common prejudices of the period is suggested by this letter Montesquiou received in 1901 from Antony Roux, who had admired the exterior of the Pavillon des Muses without knowing who inhabited it: "My God, make it be that [this residence] not belong today to a *Jew!* Obviously I have nothing against Jews, but as a Frenchman I suffer to see them set themselves up in these beautiful châteaux, these beautiful palaces that represent all the history of an elegant people who love beauty." [42]

News of the sale of the portrait was reported in *La Bavarde* on November 10, 1902, along with hints of Montesquiou's forthcoming adventures:

It is reported that the count-poet has just sold for 75,000 [*sic*] francs his portrait by Whistler.…It is not reported who acquired

73 Unknown photographer, *Dining Room of the Pavillon des Muses,* from *La Revue contemporaine,* July 25, 1901, Paris, Bibliothèque Nationale de France, Whistler's portrait of Montesquiou at right

this canvas. Perhaps it is the same *Mistress* Marbury who has just offered the noble count 175,000 francs for a three-month lecture tour in the United States. The portrait would follow, as well as some of the works of art picked up by the count's secretary, works which all of Paris marvelled at during the spring receptions the poet of hydrangeas organized at the pavilion he inhabits near the Bois de Boulogne.[43]

Back in London, Whistler continued to fume. A number of fragmentary drafts, some scribbled in pencil rather than the artist's customary elegant pen, suggest that he was planning to attack Montesquiou in the press, as he had done to others so often in the past. In deciphering these fragments, one can almost feel Whistler's rage: "Sir— We, *nous autres,* have waited to see if M. de Montesquiou would in his confidences to America, reveal his own great talent in their God gifted speciality—business!" "Sir—Monsieur le Comte de Montesquiou has hidden from you his own great talent in what he proposes is your highest quality. 'Materialism' he calls it, though…Monsieur le Comte descendant of d'Artagnan and the rest of it is…." "Monsieur le Comte de Montesquiou is well born though, as yet, not accustomed to toil. It is however true—he brings the blush to the cheek of a great family of France by commercial successes that he would himself appear in his confidences to repudiate as the practices 'materiel' & repugnant. Montesquiou, descendant of d'Artagnan, Schwashbuckler, Bucaneer…." [44]

To an unidentified party, Whistler drafted this note: "The little correspondence I send you should at once appear….It may be in time for this evening's papers…." And (in French): "Here at last are the 'pieces'— and Montesquiou's price is known—cheaper it seems than had expected the noble American—who was prepared to pay a lot more to this weak descendant of the crusades." [45] The most likely recipient of this note would have been Francis Viélé-Griffin (1864-1937), the American-born disciple of Whistler's late friend Mallarmé, who wrote the artist on March 10, 1903, that Canfield had informed him of Montesquiou's perfidy:

> M. Canfield, the lucky acquirer, informed me of the disqualifying business that Montesquiou has indulged in—it is not the only time that he has done so and, all things considered, it was good that your work should pass into clean hands. The count in question is more and more penniless—and this just when he's minting it! People talk of 170,000 francs picked up elsewhere— I don't know from what source flowed this river of gold.[46]

However much he understood Whistler's feelings, this poet attempted to dissuade him from taking his case to the press, writing:

> In any case, my dear Master, I do not think it timely, for the moment at least, to launch your anecdote: interest is elsewhere, politics are very much in the way; your Montesquiou, an avowed Barnum, is forever more beneath all criticism and the stories, similar to the one M. Canfield told me, are numerous in the life of a dealer—if any one of them, however, reached the special lowness of the Jewish act of which you were the victim.[47]

That Whistler ignored this advice and persisted in his efforts to upset Montesquiou during his American tour is suggested by these copies of correspondence preserved at Glasgow, dating from the spring of 1903:

"Sir, Whistler encloses some correspondence which he thinks should be published. It shows that Monsieur de Montesquiou has gone to lecture in America because he has a strong business sense." "Sir, Monsieur le comte de Montesquiou, descendant of d'Artagnan, has hidden from the paper his greatest quality which is materialism, and Whistler suggests this should be pointed out in their evening paper." [48] There is no evidence to suggest that Whistler's reaction to the sale was ever published, but found amidst the artist's effects after his death were newspaper clippings recounting Montesquiou's activities in New York.

Viélé-Griffin's letters to Whistler, incidently, present a most unflattering picture of how Montesquiou was viewed among progressive literary folk at this time:

> The extraordinary silliness that the ex-"*Des Esseintes*" displays, his pretension, the untellable stupidity—would scandalize if one hadn't known for a long time the mental value of the individual. A bad poet cannot be a man of taste—if this axiom needed to be demonstrated, the attitude of this ridiculous puppet would be instructive. [49]

Others, such as Ferdinand Bac in his *Souvenirs parisiens,* were more understanding of Montesquiou, and particularly of his financial needs:

> Not everything about him was noble, nor caricatural. He had a grand style that only the heirs of the old France are capable of savoring completely. But his need of money—for him who did not earn any—diminished in him that which his nature preserved in a need for ostentation. Thus his life was always refined to the highest degree but it balanced on a single pin, as unstable as his body, which, on his high heels, would bend over backwards so far that it threatened his equilibrium. [50] It should also be noted that until the death of his father in 1904, at the age of eighty, Montesquiou was living off his inheritance from his mother—what he called his "*matrimoine.*"

One individual who advised Montesquiou on selling works of art in his possession was Maurice Lobre (1862–1951), an artist who specialized in painting interiors of Versailles rather in the manner of Walter Gay. An undated letter from Lobre to the poet suggests that Lobre might have intervened at some point in selling the portrait to Canfield:

> The impression was very good in general, the Whistler basically is the only thing he would want....He is going away, he has only a little money left, he says, which is probably true, for he is an orderly type, but the desire remains. Who knows, perhaps you can make him decide when he will be home, tranquil, rested from his trip, when the expenses of Paris will be forgotten, etc.— so much for that one. [51]

Canfield returned to New York in May 1903, but he did not take possession of his own portrait or Montesquiou's for several months, as Miss Birnie Philip, after Whistler's death in July, had to arrange transfer of the canvases from Whistler's studio to the dealer W. Marchant, Goupil's successor, for delivery to the United States. She wrote of doing this to Charles Freer on July 30, 1903: "As you are about to leave London I wish to thank you for the attention that you have given to the two pictures now in the studio belonging to Mr. C[anfield]. I mean his own & that of Comte Robert. At your suggestion these pictures have been delivered to Mr. Marchant who will have the proper varnishing attended to and when the pictures are thoroughly dry, they will forward them to Mr. C's address." After asking Freer to settle a price with Canfield for Canfield's own portrait, she concluded, "I leave to yourselves the final adjustment of the price knowing that they could not be in better hands." [52] Canfield had them installed in his opulent house at 5 East Forty-fourth Street, which had served as both a residence for his family and the setting for his gambling operations until he closed down the latter in 1901. But these premises were unlike the usual sordid dens where gambling flourished. As George H. Kennedy recalled, "At Canfield's gentlemen in their evening clothes played in the atmosphere of an art gallery." [53] Shortly before Canfield's stay in London, when the District Attorney for the City of New York had led a raid on Canfield's establishment—via a second-floor window—the master of the house calmly received the police and offered them a tour, pausing to remark: "There, gentlemen, is the second largest collection of Whistler in the world [in deference to Freer's]. I am sure you all appreciate the work of this great master." [54] Canfield's biographer evoked the atmosphere of the surroundings in which the Montesquiou portrait probably hung: "The bedrooms on the fourth were all resplendent in their magnificence. Whistler oils and etchings, Chinese Chippendale furniture and Chinese porcelains of the Ching period." [55]

Canfield closed his casinos at Newport and Saratoga in 1905 and 1907 respectively, lost much of his fortune—$12,000,000—in the financial panic of 1907, but recouped it by developing a factory for the manufacture of beer-bottling machinery. All the while he continued to savor his collection of Whistlers, frequently lending them to exhibitions. The portrait of Montesquiou, for instance, appeared in Providence at the Rhode Island School of Design Museum of Art in April 1904 (as No. 2), in Boston at the Whistler memorial exhibition organized by the Copley Society in 1904 (No. 39)—from which Berenson addressed a copy of the catalogue to Montesquiou—in Philadelphia at the Pennsylvania Academy of Fine Arts' Annual Exhibition in 1907 (No. 126), in New York at the Metropolitan Museum of Art's *Paintings by Whistler* exhibition in 1910 (No. 32), and in Buffalo at the Albright Art Gallery's *Whistlers from the Canfield Collection* in 1911 (No. 2).

Finally, in the year of his death, Canfield decided to accept a longstanding proposal from M. Knoedler and Co. of New York to buy his Whistler collection. Kennedy described the transaction:

> One day in 1914 Roland Knoedler...found Canfield having a late breakfast at Delmonico's. "When are you going to sell us those Whistlers, Dick?" he asked. "You can have them today for $300,000," Canfield said. "Just a minute," Knoedler replied. He went to the telephone. "All right," he said, when he returned. "We'll send our wagon around." Knoedler must have telephoned Frick, because the next day the pictures were in Frick's house.[56]

Canfield sent Roland Knoedler's partner, Charles Carstairs, a copy of the 1911 Buffalo exhibition catalogue with an inscription dated March 9, 1914, along with a note that referred to "our talk today," probably referring to the conversation described by Kennedy.[57] Knoedler's

receipt book indicates that on March 12 the gallery bought from Canfield thirty-four Whistlers—six paintings, three pastels, and twenty-five watercolors and drawings—for a total payment of $200,000.[58] The same receipt book indicates that on March 18, 1914, Henry Clay Frick purchased *Le Comte Robert, Rosa Corder* (fig. 123), and *The Ocean* (fig. 5) for a total of $200,000, less a discount of $5,000 for payment in cash.[59] While the Knoedler accounts list only this lump sum for what Mr. Frick purchased, the collector's own record book—*Paintings and Other Works of Art Owned by Henry C. Frick*—indicates a specific price paid for each of the three works by Whistler. That given for *Comte Robert de Montesquiou-Fezensac* was $60,000,[60] almost double what Knoedler had paid Canfield for it. For recording these recent Whistler acquisitions, Mr. Frick ordered a new "Whistler" rubber stamp made for use in his account books (fig. 76), just as he previously had done for "Titian," "Rembrandt," "Vermeer," and so on.

Another American collector of the time, Robert Clark, learned of Mr. Frick's purchases and wrote from Paris about them to his son on May 4, 1914: "I would not have given over ten thousand dollars for the two portraits that Frick bought at such an enormous price and if I had I should have sold them the day after. They were so rottenly drawn that I could not have stood for them." [61]

Mr. Frick (fig. 77), however, proudly installed his new Whistler acquisitions in the house he was renting from George W. Vanderbilt (fig. 78) at 640 Fifth Avenue, until he moved them a few months later into his new residence at 1 East Seventieth Street, which he took over in the fall

75 Unknown photographer, *Arnold Seligmann with his Grandson Maxime*, c. 1931, Paris, Seligmann family

of 1914. Floor plans indicating the location of various artists' works throughout the house list "Whistler" in two locations—the stair landing on the second floor and Mr. Frick's office, which had a separate entrance on Seventy-first Street (fig. 79). From surviving photographs and descriptions of these areas of the house, it is evident that Montesquiou's portrait hung on the west wall of the office to the left of the fireplace. *Miss Rosa Corder* (fig. 123), also acquired in 1914, hung behind Mr. Frick's desk on the east wall of the office. By 1921, however, the Pennells were stating that "The *Montesquiou*…hung upstairs in his [Mr. Frick's] New York house—not with the four great Whistlers in his office." [62] After his 1914 Whistler acquisitions, Mr. Frick would acquire two more portraits by Whistler—those of Mrs. Frederick R. Leyland and Lady Meux, purchased in 1916 and 1918 respectively. Interestingly enough, the works by Whistler in Mr. Frick's office hung alongside the only other painting by an American artist that Mr. Frick judged worthy of his future museum—Gilbert Stuart's portrait of George Washington.

Henry Clay Frick died in his New York residence on December 2, 1919. His widow continued to live there until her death in 1931, after which time Mr. Frick's office was demolished during the transformation of the original Frick house into the museum that would open as The Frick Collection on December 16, 1935. On that occasion, visitors were generally pleased to find Whistler's portrait of Montesquiou hanging on the south-west wall of the newly constructed Oval Room, in a grouping with the other three Whistler portraits around Velázquez' *King Philip IV of Spain* (fig. 80). Though the *New Yorker*'s critic felt there was in The Frick Collection "Above all…too much Whistler," [63] the *New York Sun*'s critic found an amusing nuance to the Oval Room's installation:

> This [Garden Court] gives into what was once a sort of lounge and office, but has now been transformed into a small intimate gallery. Here four full-length portraits by Whistler are hung together with the great Velasquez portrait of Philip IV…giving a new and disturbing twist to the famous "Why drag Velasquez in?" [something Whistler once said when his work was being favorably compared with the Spanish master's] that the debonair Jimmy certainly never intended when he made the remark. For besides the Spaniard's serenely accomplished realization of complacent royalty, at least three of the Whistler portraits fade into vapery visions and even the fourth, the Lady Meux, which because of its lighter key holds up better, appears comparatively hesitant and uncertain. [64]

A critic writing for the *Christian Science Monitor* made an apt observation concerning the Montesquiou portrait: "Comte Robert de Montesquiou-Fezensac…presents a slender, full-length figure in fencing-master pose that curiously recalls the painter's own carriage in certain portraits," [65] probably thinking of Chase's portrait of Whistler (fig. 1). The dean of New York art critics at the time, Edward Alden Jewell, wrote in *The New York Times*:

> We accept, too, in a mood just of delighted surprise, the ingenious—no, the inspired—arrangement of pictures in the sumptuously appointed Oval Room….In cold type, this may seem, when we include the seventeenth-century Spanish

76 *Imprint from Henry Clay Frick's "Whistler" stamp,* 1914, New York, Frick Collection

77 Unknown photographer, *Henry Clay Frick,* c. 1909, New York, Frick Collection

78 Hibon, *Exterior Elevation of the Vanderbilt Houses at 640 Fifth Avenue* (detail), engraving, from E. Strahan, *Mr. Vanderbilt's House and Collection,* I, 1883, New York, Frick Art Reference Library

79 Unknown photographer, *Henry Clay Frick's Former Office Seen from Seventy-First Street,* c. 1925, New York, Frick Collection

80 D. Velázquez, *King Philip IV of Spain,* oil, 1644, New York, Frick Collection

monarch, a rather strange group. In that all but miraculous Oval Room…such juxtapositions appear really the most natural in the world. It is, you decide…just what Whistler needed—what he always needed—to give his art "body"; nor does the estimable Velasquez suffer any irreparable damage brought thus into contact with gossamer modern elegance. The once proud Whistlers, alas, grow more and more inarticulate each year. Soon, at this rate, there will be naught left of the elusive "Rosa Corder."[66]

After ten years, this installation in the Oval Room was replaced with the current Van Dyck-Gainsborough mix, and aside from a brief period in the Music Room, Whistler's portrait of Montesquiou disappeared from public view as it hung in various rooms and halls on the second floor of the museum, and even spent some time in the vault. The reason for this was not a questioning of its artistic quality, but a continuing physical deterioration that by the mid 1960s made the picture almost impossible to see. In a memorandum in the files concerning the Montesquiou portrait, it was noted in 1965:

> A number of years ago, he [William Suhr, then The Frick Collection's conservator] and Mr. Clapp [the museum's Director] discussed the condition of these pictures, the uncommon darkness, the deteriorated surface film and the bloom in the Montesquiou. A cursory test showed an extreme sensitiveness of the paint film to customary varnish solvents. The bloom was found to be between layers of varnish and not in or on the surface.

Conservation efforts were not undertaken again until 1970, when Suhr analyzed the problems as follows:

> The varnish or varnishes have added to the deplorable state of the painting. These accumulated layers have darkened and degenerated. Bloom (a cloudy appearance of aged varnish films, caused by the presence of minute cracks which diffuse light) and blanching (a milky look caused by evaporated solvents in old films) have developed between the varnish layers. The problem of restitution of this picture is to find a way of taking off the varnish and later paint additions without impairing any further the rather recent (about 90 years old) original dissolutive paint film which is already abraded. The solution seems to lie not so much in the potency of a solvent but rather in the manipulation of it—to stop its action before it reaches the original paint.

The devarnishing and removal of layers of over-paint was a lengthy procedure, but it was nothing compared to the line-by-line retouching of the myriad abraded threads of the canvas that were exposed with the removal of the opaque and discolored varnishes (fig. 81). Whistler himself had been responsible for many of these abrasions, having repeatedly wiped out his own work with washing, rubbing with pumice stone (see p. 74), and even with a razor, as Cowan had observed.[67] Notes of the conservation work began in September 1970 and went on until June 1972.[68] Suhr recalled that it was the most difficult task he had undertaken in over thirty years of looking after paintings in The Frick Collection. More recently, at the J. Paul Getty Museum, Mark Leonard

faced similar problems in conserving Whistler's *Arrangement in Black: Portrait of Señor Pablo de Sarasate* (fig. 124) and found Suhr's records a valuable help.

Once restored to something like the enamelled perfection it possessed a hundred years ago, Whistler's *Arrangement in Black and Gold: Comte Robert de Montesquiou-Fezensac* was reinstalled for some years in the Oval Room, but since 1990 it has hung in the East Gallery, along with the three others portraits by Whistler in The Frick Collection.

The Lithographs

In response to the acclaim given Whistler's portrait of Montesquiou at the Salon of 1894, there came requests for reproductions of it to be published in various periodicals. The *Figaro Salon* and *The Art Journal* were the first—just after the opening of the exhibition—as attested to by this letter from Whistler to David C. Thomson at the Goupil Gallery in London, written on Saturday, April 28, 1894:

> I saw old Valadon [of Goupil's in Paris] this morning—in answer to a note they wrote asking to reproduce my full length portrait of the Comte de Montesquiou. I don't think I like your head of the "House" [i.e., Valadon] and in any case I am not going to let them have a vulgar reproduction from this swell picture in the midst of what I told him is the "venerable" text of Monsieur Yriarte [Charles Yriarte, editor and author of the *Figaro Salon* annual for 1894]!—It was for the "Figaro Salon" they wanted it.—Indeed I have other plans and probably you will hear of them....

In a postscript, the artist added:

> Just received your letter. I shall be very pleased to have a good reproduction of the portrait of the comte in the Art Journal. But it ought to be done *exactly* like the one of Carlyle in the P. M. Budget.[1] Who do you propose to write the text? We don't want any Widmores or Spielmans or Claude Philips—Why not write to Mr. Whibley [Charles Whibley, an author who would marry Beatrice Whistler's sister Ethel Philip in the summer of 1895]? He is staying in Paris just now and his address is Hotel de France et Lorraine, *rue de Beaune.* Get him to do it.

Then Whistler appended a tiny drawing of the portrait (fig. 83) showing how he wished its reproduction to be set on the page, and noting: "The reproduction ought to be on a full page—with plenty of *white margin.* This would look much better than too big a picture with less margin."[2]

Though the page format of *The Art Journal* was narrower than indicated in Whistler's sketch (31.5 x 23.5 cm.), the photographic reproduction of the portrait that appeared in the 1894 annual publication (fig. 84) did conform closely to his wishes so far as layout was concerned, being full-page with spacious margins, a third more generous at the bottom than at the top. With Whistler's signature and butterfly emblem reproduced as well, the caption identified the image as representing "The Comte de Montesquieu [*sic*]. From the picture by J. McNeill Whistler." Unlike the text under an accompanying reproduction of *The Little White Girl,* a work of 1865 now in the Tate Gallery, London, the Montesquiou caption did not indicate who owned the painting. The image, made from a photograph Thomson had had taken at the Salon, did little credit to the original, but the painting's dark and glowing surfaces were just as difficult to photograph and reproduce then as they are now. Whistler fussed a great deal over the plate made by Badoreau from the glass negative, but ultimately he accepted a proof of it, as he reported to Thomson on September 17: "You will be pleased to hear that yesterday I 'passed,' or approved of the last proof that was brought to me of the Montesquiou portrait. I mean that, after all, it *might do.* Of course they have persisted in touching up—but still it is not so bad—and in the Journal will I daresay work pretty well."[3]

82 Whistler, *Count Robert de Montesquiou, No. 1,* transfer lithograph, 1894, New York, Paul F. Walter

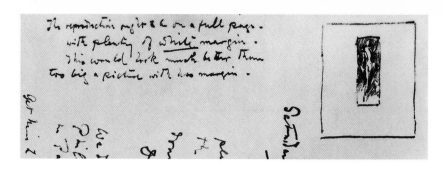

83 Whistler, *Letter to David C. Thomson*
(excerpt), April 28, 1894, Washington,
Library of Congress

The Art Journal's unsigned accompanying text—"Art and Mr.
Whistler"—was indeed the work of Charles Whibley, as Thomson
revealed in a letter to Whistler of August 14, 1894: "I am wondering too
when Mr. Whibley will send his article. If you see him could you mention
I was asking?" [4] Whibley's text clearly echoes his future brother-in-law's
ideas, as in this discussion of the Montesquiou portrait in reference to
The Little White Girl:

> If you compare his early pictures with his latest, you cannot fail
> to be struck with their unity of aim, differ as they may in the
> result obtained. It is now many years since 'The Little White
> Girl' was painted; the portrait of the 'Comte de Montesquieu'
> [*sic*] dates but from yesterday. In both there is the same simplicity
> of scheme, the same restraint in the treatment; in both there is
> the same dignity, the same grace of pose. The girl, in her flowing
> white gown, leans against the mantel, her fine head reflected in
> the mirror; the Count, in sober evening dress, stands holding
> languidly his long, light cane. For one, as for the other, the most
> limited palette has served the artist's purpose, and an arrangement
> as uncompromisingly severe as in those royal portraits by
> Velasquez, where a curtain, a chair, and a table alone enter into
> the composition.

Interestingly enough for what is to follow, Whibley went on to
announce Whistler's recent adoption of the medium of lithography:

> But, within the last few years, when he has sought to express
> himself in pure line, the lithographer's stone has appealed to him

84 Unknown photographer,
*Reproduction of Whistler's Portrait of
Montesquiou,* from *The Art Journal,* 1894,
New York, Frick Art Reference Library

85 H.-C. Guérard, *Le Comte Robert de
Montesquiou-Fezensac,* drypoint with
etching and roulette work, 1894, from T.
Duret, *Histoire de J. Mc N. Whistler et de
son oeuvre,* 1904, New York, Frick Art
Reference Library

more forcibly than the etcher's copperplate. He heralded, as it were, the revival in the art of lithography, which has had such a marked influence upon artists in Paris, and which is virtually the expression of their revolt against the encroachments of the photographer.…It is really Mr. Whistler…who has tested to greatest advantage the resources of the stone, and for lithography there is this much to be said, that it gives us his every line and touch, without the intervention of acids.[5]

The next art publication that tried to publish a reproduction of the portrait was the venerable *Gazette des Beaux-Arts.* Whistler reviewed the history of this adventure in a letter Thomson received on August 21, 1894:

They [the publishers of the *Gazette*] had asked me to let them reproduce the Count, and he also had asked. I had *agreed.* The end of it was such an infamous etching [fig. 85] by a man of distinction here that I went down in a fury and made them put it aside on the promise that I would *myself* do them an etching or lithograph. This I did my very impossible to execute [*sic*]—But I was so bored to death with it that I had to give it up after keeping them waiting. One *cannot* produce the same masterpiece twice over!! I had no inspiration—and not working at a *new* thing from nature, I found it impossible to copy *myself!*[6]

Because the relevant archives of the magazine were destroyed during World War II, it is impossible to give a full account of the *Gazette*'s approaching first Whistler and then Henri-Charles Guérard (1846-1897), the creator of the intaglio reproduction of the portrait, a drypoint with etching and roulette work.[7] But Whistler's correspondence with Thomas R. Way, Jr., the son and partner of his London lithographic printer, provides at least a partial record of the evolution of his own lithographic interpretation of the Montesquiou portrait. Way, whose responses have not been preserved, was at the time compiling his catalogue of Whistler's lithographs. In a letter dated July 6, 1894, the artist wrote him:

Now today *most important*—Am sending you drawing sketch impression of my Comte de Montesquiou—for the Gazette des Beaux Arts—Do send me proof as *soon as* possible—and then the Gazette shall have it for their edition—which, I take it, you will like to print—I hope it will turn out all right—and I rely on its simplicity though there is a little mixture of the old German chalk with the French No. 2. Directly I have your proof I shall put the Gazette people in communication with you.[8]

Though Whistler had been used to working directly on the stone to produce his early lithographs, even to the point of having the senior Way lug stones aboard barges on the Thames so that he might draw directly from his subject, by the 1890s the artist was drawing the majority of his lithographs on prepared transfer paper. Not only was paper less cumbersome and more easily portable than blocks of limestone, but images drawn with lithographic crayons on transfer paper could be mailed easily to Whistler's favorite printers in London. There the drawings would be run facedown through the press, so that the grease of the medium would be transferred onto the clean stone prepared for printing. With this procedure, the final image came out in the same direction as the artist's

original drawing. In experimenting with a wide range of transfer papers, some unfamiliar to the Ways, Whistler considerably complicated the latter's printing tasks. On July 9, he wrote Way nervously about his effort:

> Also what about the Portrait of the Comte de Montesquiou?— Do be sure to send me a line *tomorrow* that I may know that you had it safely and that it is all right!…Now as I told you, the portrait is for the Gazette des Beaux Arts—of which you would do the printing—transferred to other stones.…Can you send me a few proofs…in the early part of this week? [9]

It was Whistler's habit to require that the large edition of a lithograph planned for insertion in a magazine be run off by machine from a stone different from the one used for the artist's own impressions, which were pulled by hand. Way must have responded negatively about the printing, for Whistler's next missive, on Friday, July 13, tried to get him back on track:

> But the Gazette des Beaux Arts business is most important!— we must manage the printing—The thing to do is to take half a dozen transfers as you did for the "Whirlwind"—Above all the one first stone of course must be kept clear for my proofs— The Gazette matter I am sure you can manage more easily than you suppose—After all the stump rubbing was *very little!*— It looks perhaps a bit elaborate, but I *went over* it all with the chalk *afterwards* as well—so that I think it will print most mysteriously rich! [10]

Writing to Way two days later, Whistler's reaction to the sight of the first proofs of his lithograph (see fig. 82) was apoplectic:

> The portrait is damnable!—I dont mean the printing which is even as good as the thing to be printed was bad! and that is saying a lot!—No, my drawing or sketch, or whatever you choose, is damnable—and no more like the superb original than if it had been done by my worst and most competent enemy!— I hope to Heavens that no one has seen it—Now wipe off the stone *at once, at once!*—sending me one proof on the commonest of paper of its destroyed state—and also every other trial proof you may have taken—that I may myself burn all—There must be no record of this abomination! It is neither for catalogue [a reference to Way's above-mentioned catalogue of Whistler's lithographs] nor posterity—and only proves what the other people could never understand—that is the folly of proposing to produce the same masterpiece twice over!! Why should one— Ridiculous. Wait till you and your Father see the picture one of these days—! [11]

Writing to Way on July 17, he halted the order for destruction: "Of course no one ever to see Portrait—though for destruction may wait till further writing...." [12] But on August 14 he concluded the affair: "Destroy also at the same time the 'Montesquiou' portrait sending proof and wiping stone—The time has come to weed out all that is unworthy." [13]

Way was later to summarize the whole experience, from the printer's point of view, in his *Memories of James McNeill Whistler:*

He agreed to do a lithograph which my father was to print. He was very keen about it, and in order to be quite certain that it might be possible to print it in sufficient numbers for the magazine itself, he used the old-fashioned grained transfer paper, which he had discarded some two years before. Alas, the result was a failure; not technically, for the proofs gave exactly what he had drawn; his non-success arose from the nature of the task he had undertaken. As he expressed it, it showed the absurdity of expecting an artist to repeat his own work....It is elaborately wrought, but quite lacking in...spontaneity....Had he drawn a pen-and-ink sketch from memory, as he did of so many of his other pictures, he would probably have made something quite satisfactory. The drawing was erased from the stone at once.[14]

In July 1896, Whistler broke off with the Ways irrevocably. Fortunately, records of happier days survive in the form of a lithograph the younger Way drew of the artist, enveloped in his coat and hunched over a lithographic stone (fig. 86), and of a dramatic lithograph Whistler executed depicting the elder Way illuminated by the glow of a low gas stove (fig. 87).[15]

To satisfy the directors of the *Gazette des Beaux-Arts* after his failed attempt at a lithograph, Whistler tried to obtain a satisfactory glass negative taken from the portrait, and he also made references to a William Hole's doing an etching of it; but in fact the portrait of Montesquiou was not reproduced in the magazine until after Whistler's death, in the November 1903 issue. There Guérard's original print illustrated Pascal Forthuny's commemorative article "Notes sur James Whistler." [16] A further run of this same image, in a slightly different color ink, was tipped into the de luxe edition of Théodore Duret's *Histoire de J. Mc N. Whistler et de son oeuvre* in 1904 (fig. 85).[17] Théodore de Wyzewa's account of the Salon of 1894 for the *Gazette des Beaux-Arts* was published in June of that year—well before Whistler began his lithographic efforts. It made no reference to the Montesquiou portrait at all and only the briefest to Whistler, "so great an artist that one always takes pleasure in finding him again." [18] To illustrate Wyzewa's article, Dagnan-Bouveret's portrait of the actress Julia Bartet, engraved by Félix Jasinski, took the place that Montesquiou might have occupied.

Whistler's first attempt to reproduce Montesquiou's portrait in lithography (fig. 82) [19] was executed with both hard and soft crayons, stump (a tool used for blending tones), and scraper (to indicate the cane) on grained transfer paper known as *papier viennois.* Its characteristics were described by Smale: "The paper was relatively thick and had a heavy coating of composition on one side, which was embossed with a suitable, often mechanical grain." [20] This grain came in at least three different grades, of which Whistler used the finest for the Montesquiou lithograph. The artist's abhorrence of the resulting print led him, as we have seen, to order that the stone be erased and that evidence of this act be shown him. As a result, Way listed only eight known impressions of the image (which he had kept as his prerogative), of which Spink has traced four extant versions, not counting the cancelled proof at the Hunterian Museum and Art Gallery (fig. 91). While Whistler never specified what it was about the lithograph that so upset him, anyone can see that it failed to capture either the elegant proportions of the portrait or its luminous mystery, and that Montesquiou's right arm was rendered with anatomical whimsy.

In his despair, the artist may have been encouraged by his wife Beatrice, who had long supported his efforts with lithography, to make another attempt to reproduce the Montesquiou portrait. This second lithograph (fig. 88), printed by Lemercier in Paris most likely in 1894, was drawn with at least two different crayons on *papier végétal,* a smooth, glassy paper made in France that lacked the mechanical grain of the earlier transfer paper.[21] The artist appears to have done some work on the stone once the drawing was transferred, which would suggest, as Spink points out, that he was sufficiently pleased with the initial proofs to make slight modifications in the image. Like the first lithograph, this one reproduces the butterfly signature on the painting. In addition, the artist signed at least three examples of the print in pencil with his butterfly emblem— another indication of his approval. Spink has traced eleven impressions of the second lithograph, plus two cancelled proofs bequeathed to the Hunterian Museum and Art Gallery with the estate of Rosalind Birnie Philip.

Way, Kennedy, and Levy considered a third lithographic reproduction of the Montesquiou portrait (fig. 89) to have been executed by Whistler, but MacDonald and Spink attributed this print to Beatrice Whistler, along with a fourth version (fig. 90).[22] Described by Way as "an artist of real skill,"[23] Beatrice had exhibited her own work at the Society of British Artists in 1886 as a "Pupil of Whistler." She must have joined with her husband in his frustrated attempts to reproduce the Montesquiou portrait during the late summer or early fall of 1894. Her drawing technique is clearly distinct from that of her husband—especially in her simplified rendering of the hand, and the way in which her lines remain resolutely two-dimensional and resist coalescing to suggest either mass or space. Furthermore, the butterfly signature on the painting does not appear within the image, nor was it pencilled in by Whistler on any known examples of either print. As Spink points out, Freer, who had acquired his proof of the third lithograph from Rosalind Birnie Philip in 1904, added this marginal notation on it: "By Mrs. Whistler." Finally, neither the third nor fourth lithograph appears in the inventory of Whistler's own lithographs in his estate, though his legatee left several impressions of both images to Glasgow University.

While Beatrice Whistler's first attempt at reproducing the portrait (fig. 89) was sufficiently different from her husband's (figs. 82, 88) to arrest attention, her second one (fig. 90) was close enough to create confusion among scholars, dealers, and collectors to this day.[24] Spink came to realize that Whistler's second lithograph and both of his wife's versions were based on tracings made on transparent *papier végétal* from a photograph of the portrait and then worked up with crayons. While this procedure got around the awkward rendition of anatomy in Whistler's first try, it contributed sufficient uniformity to both husband's and wife's efforts to baffle the experts, who sometimes regarded Beatrice's second print as a later state of one of her husband's. Appropriately enough, it was Whistler himself who provided the clinching support for MacDonald's and Spink's arguments in a letter he sent Mrs. Clifford Addams in September 1901. This apprentice at the Académie Carmen had reported to the artist that

88 Whistler, *Count Robert de Montesquiou, No. 2,* transfer lithograph, 1894(?), New York, Frick Collection

89 Beatrice Whistler, *Count Robert de Montesquiou,* transfer lithograph, 1894(?), New York, Frick Collection

unauthorized impressions of the later Montesquiou lithograph were being sold in Paris. In commanding her to get his Paris lawyers on the case, Whistler remarked, "Also probably the proofs are two lithographs my wife did—far more beautiful." [25]

Robert de Montesquiou preserved until his death a large photograph of his portrait by Whistler (fig. 66), and retained as well inscribed first editions of the artist's books. In addition he possessed an impression of Beatrice Whistler's second lithograph after his portrait (fig. 90). It could possibly be the one his admirer and future biographer, the Duchesse Élisabeth de Clermont-Tonnerre, wrote to him about in 1903: "I found a drypoint [sic] by Whistler after the picture that he made of you. It is rather good without being perfect but I was very happy over this discovery made thanks to Mademoiselle Breslau [Marie-Louise-Catherine Breslau, 1856–1928, an artist friend of Montesquiou's]." [26]

91 Whistler, *Count Robert de Montesquiou, No. 1* (cancelled impression), transfer lithograph, 1894, Glasgow, Hunterian Art Gallery

90 Beatrice Whistler, *Count Robert de Montesquiou,* transfer lithograph, 1894(?), Paris, private collection, provenance Montesquiou

The Art Interpreter

Casually dropping a name or two, Montesquiou recalled in his memoirs that in 1898 he had followed the funeral procession of Gustave Moreau alongside Degas. He went on to note:

> [Degas] always annoyed me a bit by the obstinate way in which he persisted in mixing up "art critics" with *art interpreters,* among whom I class myself, for my very modest part; but when this role raises itself up to its greater possibilities, what higher recompense could there be for an artist…than the suggestions offered by his work…? [1]

Indeed, Montesquiou did excel as a commentator on and interpreter of works of art, perhaps far beyond his accomplishments as a poet. A passionate interest in the arts characterized his life from adolescence to the grave.

There was no one in the poet's immediate family to awaken his aesthetic proclivities. Rather, he recalled that this had happened spontaneously one day during a break in his classes at the Collège de l'Immaculée Conception:

> One fine day—yes, truly, one fine day!…a prophetic chance made me walk alone [and] *I perceived a rose…*and then—which was more important—to prove to me that in spite of my insecurity, even the ferocity of families, the stupidity of knowledge and the godlessness of religions, [I discovered] *that there was Beauty on this Earth.* [2]

This revelation was immediately compounded by another that would equally mark the boy for life:

> One of my companions in captivity, who was passing by and to whom I had never spoken, encountered my glance, shared the ecstasy of it…picked the flower, and without saying a single word, [he gave it to me] and I understood *that there was Friendship on this earth.* [3]

Montesquiou's budding sensibilities manifested themselves first in certain decorative arrangements in his own rooms—as when he suspended over a "barbarous" corner cabinet a large glass bowl containing a goldfish—but the young man soon realized that these tendencies would lead no further than to what he called "the decorator's manner…which does not aspire very high and comes to a halt quite soon." [4] Instead, encouraged by Lucien Doucet (see fig. 21), he sensibly enrolled in classes at the Académie Julian in the mid 1870s. This institution, founded by Rodolphe Julian in 1868, offered an alternative art training less rigorous than that of the traditional École des Beaux-Arts. Open to all who applied—men and women—for whatever time they chose to enroll, its professors trained students in the basics of drawing, painting, and sculpture. The studios, in Montesquiou's day, were located in the passage des Panoramas, near the Bourse. The future poet recorded his association with the academy in a few words: "I started to frequent the Académie Julian, whence emerged quite a few celebrated mediocrities, among whom I will not even class myself, because I achieved no success and withdrew quickly." [5] Montesquiou's name in fact appears nowhere among the rather complete archives of the Académie Julian. [6]

However long he attended the school, Montesquiou must have learned there the essential techniques that enabled him throughout his life

92 P. Helleu, *Devant les Watteau du Louvre,* drypoint, c. 1895, Paris, private collection, first proof

to draw his friends and contemporaries with caricatural verve (see fig. 93), to convey his joy in contemplating his favorite flowers (fig. 30), or— perhaps in homage to Whistler—to evoke the mysterious beauties of Venice (fig. 94). Toward the end of his memoirs, the poet looked back soberly on this body of work:

> This lode comprises about two hundred drawings undertaken by me, from the time when the desire to give a form to my ideas and my feelings hesitated between contours and characters. I do not think I took the wrong direction in devoting myself entirely to letters, nor do I believe that I wasted the time employed in noting, with a few attentive touches, certain effects of nature or in interpreting with my own compositions certain favorite texts.[7]

He showed his paintings only to a few individuals, but after his death over a hundred of them were exhibited in 1923 at the Galeries Georges Petit in an exhibition patronized by the Comtesse Greffulhe. In the catalogue's introductory text, Arsène Alexandre, once Montesquiou's bitterest adversary, suggested certain parallels between the poet's verbal and visual effects, noting that "these watercolors of Montesquiou enable us to connect their color harmonies with the fiery glow of precious stones that he transposed so brilliantly into words and rhymes." [8]

In addition to developing at the Académie Julian the modest skills that he employed in his own work, Montesquiou must also have absorbed there sufficient understanding of the principles of design and the nature of creative invention for him to examine the work of superior artists with understanding. He also assembled over the years an impressive art library with a large collection of photographs that served as reference sources for his own writings. This art interpreter published books, catalogues, articles, and extensive passages in his memoirs devoted to the following painters, sculptors, and craftsmen, along with comments on many other artists along the way: Bakst, Beardsley, Besnard, Blake, Boecklin, Boldini, Bresdin, Breslau, Burne-Jones, Carriès, Chassériau, Gallé, Grandville, Guys, Helleu, Ingres, Jacquet, Lalique, László, Lemaire, Leonardo, Monticelli, Moreau, Rodin, Rouveyre, Sargent, Stevens, Tissot, Troubetzkoy, Vernet, Watteau, and, of course, Whistler.[9] The impact Montesquiou made upon his contemporaries with these texts is suggested by a journalist who lamented the poet's leaving the Pavillon des Muses in 1909, citing "twenty years of a new and personal art that Robert de Montesquiou patronized, imposed on others, deified through his writings, and of which certainly the most extraordinary of our contemporaries will remain as the initiator and the incarnation." [10]

Given the focus of the present book, it would be impossible to analyze Montesquiou's writings on all of the artists cited above, or to discuss his personal relationships with many of those concerned, but it seemed appropriate to assemble here a selection of reproductions of works by a few of the artists under consideration and to pair these with excerpts from Montesquiou's writings—as though putting together an album of the sort the art interpreter appreciated so.

93 Montesquiou, *Eight Portrait Studies,*
graphite, pen and ink, after 1887(?), Paris,
private collection, clockwise: Marcel
Proust, Prince Edmond de Polignac,
Charles Haas, Gabriel Yturri, Charles
Hawkins, Pranzini (a triple murderer)

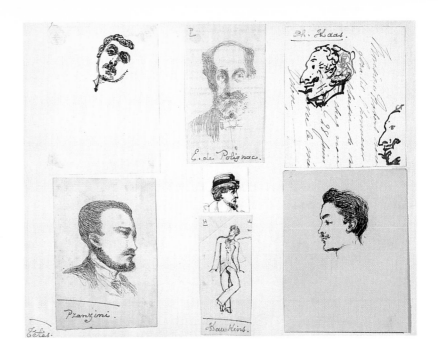

94 Montesquiou, *Venice,* watercolor,
n.d., Paris, private collection

Giovanni Boldini
(1842–1931)

Yes, Parisianism, Modernity, *these are the two words inscribed by the Ferrarese Master [Boldini] on each leaf of his tree of knowledge and of grace. A tree that tempts all Eves lacking a portrait, all the Sphinxes of the studio, whose enigma, through a hundred fine pictures, makes variations on the two smart words:* modernity, Parisianism. *Parisianism, something like 'The State' in 'The State of Elegance': something more Parisian than Paris, as what one could call Tanagrism was more Athenian than Athens. In other words…the collusion of flesh and fabric, which molds or masks, promises or denudes, prettifies, in a pose, an arm emerging from a sleeve, like a garland of flowers; or, beneath the ruffles, makes a foot thrust out, like the beak of a bird. Modernity, the secular reminder of the date through attire, that was the string of pearls of a Coello, the ruff of a Pourbus, the pucker of cloth of a Watteau; that will be a certain bolero of Boldini, a certain drapery of Besnard, an evening wrap of Whistler.*[11]

Boldini
Robert de Montesquiou considère la canne
Qui vient de Louis Quinze et d'Edmond de Goncourt
L'instrument tient du luth et de la sarbacane,
L'harmonie y murmure et le sarcasme y court.[12]
(see fig. 95)

Rodolphe Bresdin
(1822–1885)

He was, in a way, a Monticelli of India ink, this Rodolphe Bresdin. After the grinder of flowers, the grinder of black. He replaces the multitude of touches of the brush with an infinity of strokes of the pen, and so offers us, in place of a canvas marvelously flecked with brilliant yarns, a canvas unbelievably tangled with dark threads.…

Among religious subjects, Bresdin seems to have preferred above all the Flight into Egypt. He doubtless saw in it his own dream of familial travel rendered divine.

I possess, in different sizes, in successive states…six variations on this theme. The play of sky against water, rocks, and especially boughs, modulates around the haloed group in linear symphonies. The two most beautiful are quite different in appearance: one, peaceful, amid the luxuriance of an Oriental vegetation, beneath the knotty intersection of branches covered with leaves; the other one (a proof in velvety black that Bresdin himself christened The Strong One*) sad, in a winter landscape, beneath the wrought iron of naked boughs, an image of death, over a torrent, image of life.…*

And the visitor, often charmed, always fascinated before the revelation of these drawings whose only equivalent are certain mediumistic markings, these drawings that one understands better in knowing that the artist sometimes sat for long hours contemplating spiders weaving their webs, that visitor will stare in wonder anew in recalling the one who was the Ixion of the lithographic stone.[13] (see fig. 96)

95 G. Boldini, *Count Robert de
Montesquiou,* oil, 1897, Paris, Musée
d'Orsay, given to the Musée du Jeu de
Paume in 1922 by Henri Pinard

96 R. Bresdin, *The Flight into Egypt,*
lithograph, 1855, Art Institute of
Chicago, provenance Montesquiou

Émile Gallé
(1846–1904)

These noble images came back to my mind while visiting with…Gabriele D'Annunzio the retrospective exhibition of Émile Gallé installed in the Musée Galliéra.…[D'Annunzio's eyes] looked down on the glistening or mat sides, the rough or polished inner surfaces of the vases, tall and slim or squat and stocky, along which run, slide, creep, stretch out, twist together, mingled with texts that comment upon them, wisteria, poppies, passionflowers, asters, Mary-hearts, iris, orchids, sage, spikes of flowers, pine needles, satin-flowers, meadow saffron, violets, gourds, bamboo, algae, rockweed and seaweed, on which clamber snails, on which flutter dragonflies, butterflies, and bats, from which jump grasshoppers and frogs, fly over or land swallows from Ornitio, hurried and with their tails forked. And, within the molten glass, a red vein has occasionally run through, like the rosy thread that recalls the need to triumph, or the necessity of dying. It was in a Berlin museum, as we know, that our man from Nancy [Gallé] saw those pieces of Chinese glass, which he admired and which served as models for him, with their superimposed vitreous layers of different colors, of which his polishing lathe, his drill, and his rivetting die would go to find, as in prepared onyx or natural cameos, the veins that would lend themselves to his own designs and from which would profit his fantasy. Oh! how Gallé surpassed the masters of the Far East, whose richly toned but unsubtle covers sheathed sumptuous and hard looks, to which the tender or somber colorations of the French glassmaker victoriously oppose the inexhaustible scale of their palette, the profound and joyous suggestions of their rainbow keyboard! [14] (see figs. 97, 98)

97 Cristallerie d'Émile Gallé, *Vase,* blown and engraved glass, marquetry, c. 1900, Norfolk, Virginia, Chrysler Museum

98 É. Gallé, *Bat Lamp,* overlay carved glass and bronze, n.d., Scarsdale, New York, Dotty and Steve

Constantin Guys
(1802–1892)

Certainly, it would be something far more than presumptuous, supererogatory, vain, and superfluous, to align lines under the name of Constantin Guys, after Baudelaire's article ["Le Peintre de la vie moderne," 1863], the most adequate of studies that has ever been devoted to an artist…if there were not occasionally a usefulness and an interest—without speaking of the attention recalled to a subject forgotten by some, unknown to many—in drawing some conclusions and in verifying some oracles.…To the names that Baudelaire cited in reference to Guys, it would be appropriate to add that of Whistler; certain delicate contests of shadow and light on a passing sheet deserving to evoke the admirable art of the master of arrangements in grey. Those others of Goya, for certain juxtapositions of black and pink.…But the early [elegant women] are more numerous in Guys' oeuvre, with their turbans *and their* bonnets, *their* bonnet strings *and their* hatpins, *their* lace tuckers *and their* bertha collars, *their* flounces *and their* canezous, *their shawls and their muffs, and as if applying themselves to the reality of a prestidigitation of the highest sort to prove that Eve can extract herself from these disproportionate and monstrous accessories; and that Venus knows how to be born from a wave of muslin and from the foam of organdy.…*

White outfits, foamy, frothy, as though beaten and whipped up like cream, in victorias and under overhanging trees, Guys excels with them. And these lead us to that predilection of the artist, what he loved no doubt as much as women: the vehicle, *the* carriage. *Not only those barouches and those dorsays, those phaetons and those tilburys, those ducs and those half-ducs, those breaks, those pony-carts and those spider buggies, whose anatomies he draws so lovingly, the elipse of the wheels, the radiant rims like rays of swiftly moving suns; whose flowery subtleties he paints with tenderness: the yellow of primulas, periwinkle blue; not only that cabriolet of the Duke of Brunswick, by which as a child I was terrified to see glowing within the turned-up greatcoat the eyes of the bogeyman in the frizzed wig like that of the archers of the palace of Darius; or yet again those large coupés like those of the queen at Windsor, a sort of carriage with seats in covers trimmed with passementerie and mounted with giants in powdered wigs and gold-laced coats, the latest examples of which were offered us in front of the church of Saint-Philippe-du-Roule for the Uzès-Luynes wedding.*[15] *(see figs. 99, 100)*

99 C. Guys, *Two Ladies Taking a Walk,*
brush and black, blue, and brown wash,
pen and black ink, n.d., New York,
Metropolitan Museum of Art,
provenance Baudelaire, Nadar

100 C. Guys, *Women in a Carriage,*
graphite, pen and brown ink, black and
grey wash, n.d., New York, Pierpont
Morgan Library

Paul Helleu
(1859–1927)

I don't think that the magnanimous artist had any troubling thoughts concerning my profile, the night that preceded the fortunate day when his famous diamond [his drypoint instrument] assured him of its endurance, for nothing of all that had been arranged; on the contrary, it was impromptu, sudden, irresistible.

It was shortly after the reading I gave, at the Pavillon des Muses, for some forty eminent friends, of a chapter of my book devoted to the memory of my companion of twenty years [Le Chancelier de fleurs]. Of that group of friends, Helleu appeared among the first. He gave me, that memorable day, during a visit I paid him, a new and remarkable proof of his friendship. I should like to describe here how much it touched me and how grateful I remain for it.

I had been in the drawing room for about a minute, before the host had appeared. Then suddenly he burst into the room, coming from the balcony, where I couldn't see him, and even without greeting me, he cried, as if in the throes of a violent inspiration: "Sit down there, Montesquiou, I want to do your portrait; for a long time Yturri had wished for it; I want to satisfy this desire of that man of whom you spoke so nobly in your work, and for whom I had a real friendship."

I felt so surprised, and at the same time so touched; I didn't know what to say. Several hours later, the etching [sic], which I regard as one of Helleu's masterpieces, was completed. Rarely are the proud satisfied with their images. I was with mine. At once youthful and aged, like the model himself perhaps, it brings out two traits of the latter's character, in whom a certain gaiety is coupled with a meditative spirit, and who seems to see emerging from this elegant and pensive interpretation, the corrected image, which makes one smile, and, at the same time, the reality, which makes one weep.[16]

As for blue hydrangeas, I have them here before my eyes; they are, along with our common love for "Palmyra, where Royalty sleeps"[Versailles], one of the predilections of Nature and of Art that unite me with the painter. "I wished it had been you who executed this portrait of me," he said again yesterday, "we love the same flowers and the same stones!" In paintings and pastels, I own seven pictures of hortensias gardened by Helleu, whose clusters, blue-green or yellowing, give off reflections, on silver platters, like bouquets of dead turquoises.[17]

At most, three or four attempts at male portraits in this innumerable collection:... Whistler, like a humorous tiger cat, one clear eye behind the monocle, the other sparkling with malice.[18] *(see figs. 101, 102, 19)*

101 P. Helleu, *Portrait of Robert de
Montesquiou,* drypoint (inscribed
to Montesquiou), 1913, Paris, private
collection, first proof

102 P. Helleu, *Hydrangeas and Bats,*
pastel, n.d., London, Nevill Keating
Pictures, Ltd., provenance Montesquiou

Adolphe Monticelli
(1824–1886)

This was a real bon vivant, a warm-hearted parent, a tried and tested friend, an artist both idealistic and sensual, one who heartily enjoyed his bouillabaisse, whose methods he did not hesitate to apply to a number of his paintings....His palette included twenty-seven colors. Anything was acceptable as a means of distributing them onto the canvas, including the stem of his pipe....But the best pictures to relate to those of this astonishing colorist we all, as children, made them ourselves, and I can see them again in my memory. In the heat of summer, we used to crush, between a board and a piece of window pane, lobelias, calceolarias, geraniums, all the most garish colors of the garden, and we happily spent hours contemplating, fascinated, these dazzling compositions conceived like this and composed of crushed flowers.[19] (see fig. 103).

103 A. Monticelli, *Under the Trees at the Water's Edge*, oil, 1883-85, New York, Mrs. Alex Lewyt

Gustave Moreau
(1826–1898)

And yet the cry that he had uttered, very shortly before his last breath, had been only a tender call of his art, nobly, curiously recapitulatory of a whole life: "I have found an admirable costume for a Salome," he had said to his friend, the morning after one of those last nights given to the final combat. And he had drawn with an emaciated and luminous finger, within the contours of a tunic, something like an imprisonment of signs and foliated scrolls, which it seemed he had gone out, that very night, beyond his insomnia and into the Invisible, to take up the mysterious outlines, to trace the cabalistic meanderings.[20]

His theory [in reference to Henri Rupp, first curator of the Musée Gustave Moreau in Paris] is to exclude nothing, and by exhibiting certain sheets and certain panels lacking in meaning for the general public, to teach artists and other interested folk about the audacity of his master, about his right to rival those colorists considered outrageous, even to surpass them in what was believed to be their excesses, finally to teach us about his working methods. It would be reckless, and no doubt harmful, to suggest that, like a glassmaker who draws inspiration from the unexpected veins of his colored crystals for the final engraving of the vase they streak, Gustave Moreau himself could well have occasionally drawn the subject of a composition out of a mess of colors, more or less accidentally intermingled on a canvas or a sheet of paper, and which revealed to him their meaning afterwards. Yet this is indeed an impression that results from certain preparations, which are no more than drippings of color of which some people could make neither head nor tail, although they might be precisely the first hint and seed of The Head and the Tail of the Serpent.[21]

Gustave Moreau
L'art des ruissellements d'irradiations,
Nul autre que Moreau ne sut ce qu'il déferle;
Et c'est l'être chargé des médiations
Entre l'onde et le feu, le rubis et la perle.…

La Salomé qu'arrête une stupeur du sang
Dont Hérode paîra sa danse dulcisone;
Et l'Hélène debout dans le soir qui descend
Sur les morts infinis que sa beauté moissone.[22]
(see figs. 104, 105, 106)

104 G. Moreau, *Study for Salomé Contemplating the Head of John the Baptist,* pen and ink, n.d., Paris, Musée Gustave Moreau

105 G. Moreau, *Abstract Sketch,* oil, n.d., Paris, Musée Gustave Moreau

106 G. Moreau, *Helen of Troy before the Scaean Gate,* oil, c. 1881, Paris, Musée Gustave Moreau

Auguste Rodin
(1840–1917)

I was saying to the Master, that work [The Soul and the Body] *seemed to me, along with his* Orpheus, *to offer admirable subjects for a mausoleum. It would give me pleasure to see Rodin devote several of his most appropriate pieces to this usage as tombs, which are almost always left to banal supernumeraries. Noble myths would embody with grandeur the terrifying mystery of certain inventions of Blake, the spirits of the departed, and the forces of Destiny. It is sad to think that there will be no Maecenas to give Rodin this gigantic expiatory commission of some magnificent cenotaphs, for which one would easily find a use, to honor certain grand and unknown dead.*

    Vast vitrines [at Rodin's studio in Meudon] *are full of fragments: clenched hands, convulsive gestures, masks, torsos; I repeat, an entire valley of Jehoshaphat of body parts ready to be rejoined into anatomies full of thought and life, when the lord of the manor, Auguste Rodin, will sound reveille with his formidable trumpet.*[23] (see fig. 107)

107 A. Rodin, *Head of John the Baptist,* bronze, 1887, Art Museum, Princeton University

John Singer Sargent (1856–1925)

108 J. S. Sargent, *Madame X (Mme Pierre Gautreau)*, oil, 1884, New York, Metropolitan Museum of Art

Swedenborg asserts that Roman Catholics, arriving in Heaven, hurry about seeking the saints for whom they had a special veneration, and are often quite astonished not to find them there.—Posterity, and if you wish, museums, are the Heaven of Art. It is possible that an art lover of today, brought back in several centuries, would be a bit surprised not to find in the picture-galleries of that time as many Sargents as he would have imagined today. But this is the secret of the future....

*By what mystery, other than that of the total power of a fascinating model...can one explain that the author of this gracious portrait [*Lady with a Rose, *New York, Metropolitan Museum of Art] could, a few years later... produce veritably, this time, a sort of masterpiece, that impressive and unforgettable portrait of Madame Gauthereau [i.e., Mme Pierre Gautreau, known as the portrait of* Madame X *], which appears in the artist's career as a culminating point, unique, accomplished from the beginning, and, since, pursued in vain, or left aside in favor of brilliant variations and facile effects, so perfectly lacking in what constituted the mystery, and almost the giddiness of that older canvas.*

If ever Enigma merited the name of Cruel*...it surely was that adventure of a painter, at the start of his career, seizing, from the grasp in which the strange beauty of a model held him, the occasion to produce a magisterial work. Then, the whole rest of the story turning to the inverse of all that one could have imagined: the lady furious, the public mocking, and the painter indignant, abandoning forever the country that witnessed his mortification....If the young artist, at that solemn hour, had derived from his apparent failure, instead of a juvenile, almost a childish spite, the pride that was appropriate, his career would have offered, I won't say an endless number of works equal to the one in question, but at least some other examples....*

I know few stories as painful as those of artists...whose self-esteem prevents them from extracting from such a trial the advantages that it intended for them; that is, asperity and pugnacity, which give to their life, as to their work, an allure of revolt and of defiance that constitutes its originality, for a future that is not always to be kept waiting indefinitely.[24] *(see fig. 108)*

Alfred Stevens
(1823–1906)

It is not impossible, some day, when all the phases of his renown have been fulfilled, that our painter will be called the master of the letters, *just as there was* the master of the carnations, *an old Swiss artist [the "Master of the Carnation," active c. 1490–1510]. Some superficial observers have criticized Alfred Stevens' pictures for lacking subjects, because he painted neither battles nor shipwrecks, in short, none of those compositions that Baudelaire groups in the category of "stationary furors." Rather the eternal feminine fallen prey to her perpetual amorous anxiety, composing a love letter, sending it off, writing it, waiting for one, receiving it, crumpling it, with all the corresponding expressions in pose and dress that emotion required, motivated: what more dramatic combats, what more poignant drownings?…The same model posed for another picture of lesser dimensions:* Memories and Regrets, *a title that well suggests its period and its fruit. Because it is an autumn fruit, this full-bodied beauty. By the arm of the chair she fills with her ample curves, it is less between the lines of the open note in her hand than among the lines of her maturing forms that she spells out herself the autumnal title of her effigy. A rare canvas, perhaps unique in Stevens' oeuvre for the enlargement of the manner and the softening of the matter that link it, on the one hand, to Degas and his inspired rendering of reality, and, on the other, to Manet, in that ivory-like depiction of flesh of which* Olympia *is the prototype. The general harmony of the garments, of the abandoned hat, discreetly flowered in russet tones, the folded parasol, lightly trimmed in blue, is all in this pale grey color of putty that should be called* Stevens grey, *and which the flesh tones illuminate softly, like a reflection of coral on silver or the sight of a late-blooming rose in the mist of the first cold days. Certain golden highlights are perhaps not entirely natural in that hair so skillfully dressed and now coming undone a bit, an ample head of hair all mounted in knots. The heavy face weighs down on the neck. The lowered glance that hovers over the letter passes over her breasts, pressing out of a blue corset of a semi-virtuous middle-class woman. The foot, too tiny and plump, is shod in a slipper that is elegant but didn't come from the very finest maker, and the ribbed lisle stocking is of the same grey, striped in blue, that makes it match with the parasol in a slightly provincial effort at refinement. Nothing here of Stevens' real ladies of the world, of those women of his family he represented in their distinguished and opulent "at homes" or whom he asked to pose for him (so that he could represent them visiting themselves), with their hat from Mme Ode, their gown from Soinard, their authentic Indian cashmere shawl. No: this one is the woman of forty in the feminine comedy of Alfred Stevens.…And it is a poignant and fascinating anomaly offered by a study of this picture, which does not have the scent of light cologne but of patchouli, and in which the slightly lusty guilelessness that emanates from the model both competes and harmonizes with the exquisite and great distinction that it derives from the art of the master.*[25] (see fig. 109)

109 A. Stevens, *Memories and Regrets,* oil,
c. 1875, Williamstown, Massachusetts,
Sterling and Francine Clark Art Institute,
provenance Montesquiou

James Tissot
(1836–1902)

There occured in the year 1894, among other singularities, a phenomenon insufficiently commented upon and truly extraordinary. Right from the beginning of the month of May, one saw clergymen heading off in the direction of the Champ de Mars. At first it was done discreetly, almost indirectly: one priest, then two. Soon the clergyman appeared to replace the military man who peoples this area. Finally the black iris of cassocks took over the blue cornflowers, the red poppies, and the golden ears of corn of the uniforms by which the avenue de la Bourdonnais habitually sees itself transformed into a walking harvest. No new sanctuary being erected in this neighborhood, no recently sanctified body displaying its relic here, then where was this religious group headed? And it was the surprise of the insufficiently informed gawker to see the obscure wake of this pious flow disappear through the entrance of our new Salon of painting.…M. James Tissot, all alone, with his revelation of the life of Our Lord Jesus Christ, had succeeded in performing this miracle: the clericalization of the Société Nationale des Beaux-Arts.…

Now, the most beautiful of these sheets? A choice that is not at all easy.…One of the most astonishing studies in foreshortening rises up in that other page without precedent in the history of painting: What Our Savior Saw from the Cross; *so astonishing that one might well ask whether the masters of an age of greater faith would not have judged it blasphemous to so objectify oneself in the persona of the Son of God, who, without any doubt, saw something quite different. Nevertheless the humanity of Christ could have, must have had some such vision, and I do not think that the erudite draughtsmanship of M. Tissot blazes anywhere else with such mastery as in this surprising sheet.…*

But The Forum, Site of the Gabbatha *is probably the masterpiece of this exhibition. It seems that Catherine Emmerick [Anna Katharina Emmerick, 1774–1824, a mystic], certainly the divine, inspiring muse for the creator of this magnificent life of Our Lord Jesus Christ, could have thus indicated the components of the scene; but, once again, can all of art explain such a rendition, or make comprehensible such a hand?* [26] (see figs. 110, 111)

110 J. Tissot, *The Forum of Jerusalem as Seen from Above*, gouache, n.d., Brooklyn Museum

111 J. Tissot, *What Christ Saw from the Cross*, gouache, c. 1888, Brooklyn Museum

The Garb

While one visitor to the Salon of 1894 was heard to comment before Whistler's portrait of Montesquiou, "Look, a suit for thirty-nine francs!," [1] more perceptive viewers recognized in this mysterious work yet another manifestation of the dandyism that had flavored French intellectual life throughout the nineteenth century. The critic Gustave Geffroy, for instance, immediately saw a link between the artist and his subject in this regard, writing:

> The creator of such beautiful silent portraits…must have been tempted, given his own dandyism, by the dandyism of Monsieur de Montesquiou. He loved what is natural and what is willed in this allure, this role so easily and so elegantly assumed, this way of life that can flourish only in periods of advanced civilization. [2]

Others who examined the portrait spoke of "a certain dandyism in the features and in the pose," [3] or saw the work as "singularly expressive in its jaunty dandyism," [4] or found "a whole sense of character, of dandyism, of intellectual taste." [5] Finally, the anonymous critic of *Gil Blas* struck a philosophical chord when he observed that Whistler "has noted these refined elegances of the dandy who wears the depressing evening suit of the common herd like court dress," [6] recalling this familiar passage from Baudelaire's "Salon de 1846":

> And yet, does it not possess its own beauty and its own indigenous charm, this evening suit so often victimized? Is it not the necessary garment for our time, suffering and wearing on its dark and skinny shoulders the symbol of perpetual mourning? Observe carefully that the black evening suit and the frock coat possess not only their political beauty, which is the expression of universal equality, but even more their poetic beauty, which is the expression of the public soul;—an immense parade of mourners, political mourners, mourners in love, middle-class mourners. We are all going to some funeral. [7]

It was the same Baudelaire, briefly a luxuriant dandy himself, who best defined the nature of the beast in his celebrated essay of 1863, "Le Peintre de la vie moderne": "Dandyism is not, as many unreflecting people seem to believe, an immoderate taste for dress and material elegance. Those things for the perfect dandy are only a symbol of the aristocratic superiority of his mind [and] only the exercises proper for strengthening the will and disciplining the soul." [8]

Such was certainly the significance Montesquiou attached to his elaborately studied appearance, and specifically to the way he chose to be portrayed by Whistler. The nature of his clothing was only another manifestation of the aesthetic preoccupations that dominated his life, whether it be his handwriting, the decoration of his residences, the selection of his letter papers, or the binding of his books. His choices in the area of haberdashery were so relentlessly extraordinary that he became the delight of cartoonists (see figs. 46, 47, 113) and the subject of journalists' comments, sometimes merely observant—"dressed in the conventional swallow-tail, with those typical short flaps always worn by the model" [9]— but sometimes mercilessly mordant:

> …in the crowd, however, a real Boldini, the poetic Comte Robert de Montesquiou-Fezensac, of a thinness and inimitable exquisiteness of forms, wearing a suit of fog or blotting-paper grey, the

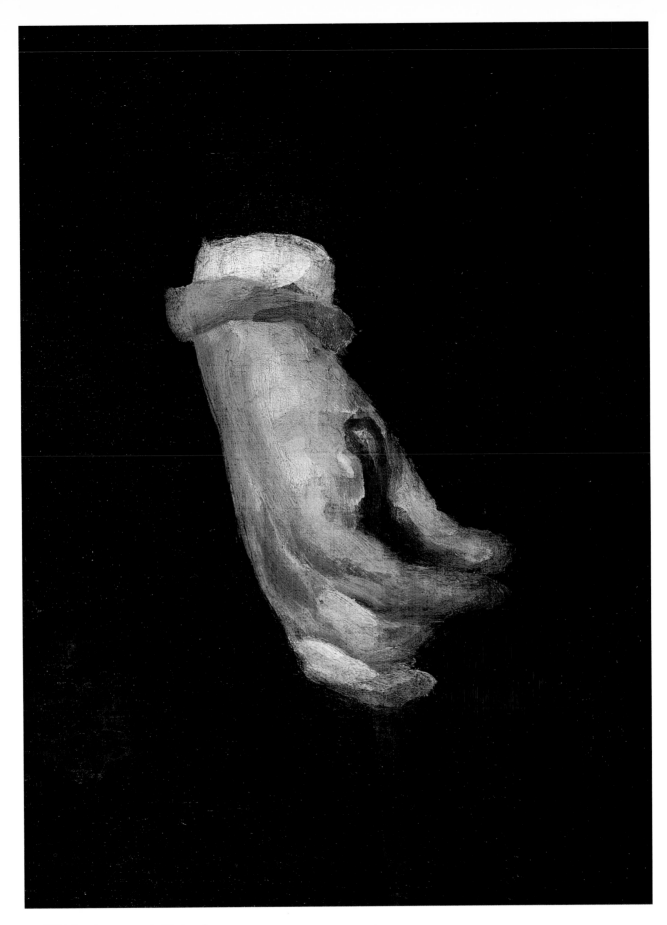

112 Whistler, *Arrangement in Black and Gold: Comte Robert de Montesquiou-Fezensac* (detail), oil, 1891–92, New York, Frick Collection

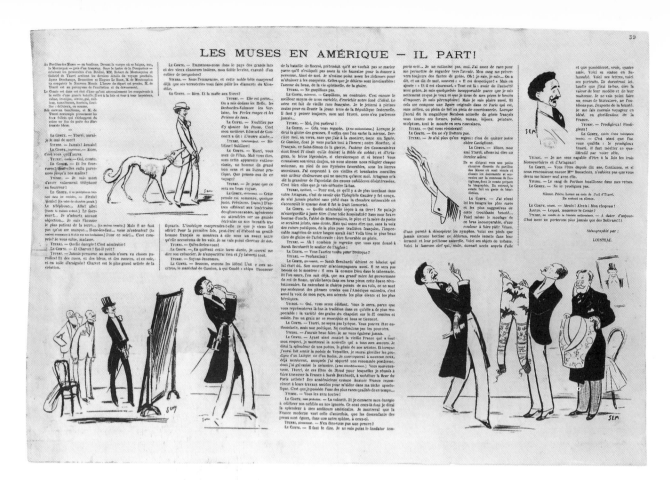

113 Sem, *Les Muses en Amérique—
Il Part!,* from *La Vie parisienne,* January
1903, Paris, Bibliothèque Nationale de
France

nuance and cut of a charming pretension; obviously Boldini
is just the man who could render that fleeting silhouette of the
most elegant des Esseintes.[10]

For the press, what Montesquiou wore at home was as interesting
as what he wore when participating in a duel: "He wears suits of clothes
of the most delicate hues, lined and faced with silk of the most exquisite
colours. The colour of the clothes is always in keeping with the general
scheme of decoration of the room in which he may be passing the day."[11]
Another commentator watched as "the Comte de Montesquiou [removes]
his dark frock coat and white waistcoat [and puts on] white gloves."[12]

Sympathetic observers saw the full-dressed Montesquiou as
someone outside their own time—"some Apollo of mystery…a being of
ages long past and who is not subject to our judgments."[13] For this
reason, the caricaturist Sem advised an imaginary provincial not to ape
dandies such as Montesquiou: "Don't try…to copy the special and
extravagant chic of that exceptional elite, of those fashion heroes who can
be allowed and pardoned such fantasies because of their personality."[14]

Even Montesquiou's obituaries made reference to his sartorial
obsessions, including Henri de Forge's observation that "each fold of
his tie too was knowingly adjusted, and the exposed portion of his shirt
cuff was calculated to the millimeter."[15]

The many photographs, both professional and informal, for
which Montesquiou posed—the Duchesse de Clermont-Tonnerre calculated 189 times—provide ample evidence of his concern for the design
and fit of his clothes. Surprisingly, he left few statements on the subject,

except for some references in his manuscript "*Théorie du serviteur, divisée en règle générale du service quotidien avec renvois par lettres aux observations particulières et par chiffres aux observations générales,*" intended to serve as a manual for his staff. There, for example, he commanded his valet "never to clean shoes without their trees inside." [16]

No elements of Montesquiou's clothing have survived, nor is much known about his tailors or other suppliers. An exception is the haberdasher Charvet, referred to by the artist Lobre in a letter he sent Montesquiou on the eve of the latter's trip to the United States in 1903: "Charvet can create marvels for you, because I know Charvet, and he said so. He has the knack of making up *waistcoats* for me that are masterpieces from the back, the front, from above, and from below. Never have I been so encased in silk, just like a bouquet of flowers!" [17] Around the same time *La Vie parisienne* published a humorous article about Montesquiou's sartorial preparations for his American journey and cited an imaginary conversation between him and Yturri:

> The count: And Charvet? Is he ready?
> Yturri: Never has anyone in the world seen such things! Rose-colored ones, and blue, and mauve, in silk, and in spiders' webs! Charvet is the greatest artist in creation. [18]

By the 1890s, Whistler's generalizing concept of the portrait precluded the sort of detailed depiction of clothing that Ingres, say, provided at an earlier period, or that an artist such as Bonnat would feature in Whistler's own day (see fig. 130). All the same, Montesquiou's portrait, through its very subtlety, tells a lot about the subject's concept of dress. In a feat of prestidigitation, Proust, utilizing his familiarity with Montesquiou's appearance to invest the personage of the Baron de Charlus, made one reference back to Whistler almost as though he had Montesquiou's portrait in mind: "I had all the leisure…to admire the intentional and artistic simplicity of his evening clothes which, by little nothings that only a dressmaker would have discerned, had the air of a 'Harmony' in black and white by Whistler." [19]

Beginning at the top, Whistler rendered faithfully Montesquiou's noble forehead from which arose the full head of thick hair of which he was justly proud (cf. fig. 114). Unlike most of his contemporaries who parted their hair in the middle, from an early age he wore his mounted high, no doubt employing the skills of an expert hairdresser. Eventually he would resort to dyeing it, and Paulette Helleu recalled that it had turned completely white in his late years.

Ferdinand Bac left a characteristically savage evocation of the poet's hair:

> His hair, waved and teased artfully into rows of curls, came to an end, one might say with the regret of not going any higher. Was not this yet another relic of the century when gentlemen fought among themselves as to who would have the most beautiful wig? His hair was like the summit of that pride that started with his heels and concluded with the curve of his *offended mane.*[20]

At least one obituary made reference to the poet's hair "set straight and very high above his forehead," adding of his important moustache and the tuft of hair below his full lower lip: "his moustache *à la française* [gave] him the air of a musketeer." [21] That writer may have been alluding to Montesquiou's forebear d'Artagnan. Indeed, the poet's adoption of this style of moustache was probably a conscious recall of his ancestor, one that dated back at least to the 1870s (cf. fig. 24). Such moustaches, very popular at the time, were set and curled with irons. They were considered to give gentlemen a martial air. In more recent times, Salvador Dalí affected a remarkably similar waxed and turned-up moustache. Whether he was inspired by Montesquiou's example is not known, but he was sufficiently aware of the poet's fame to have owned one of his celebrated canes—though not, as often reported, the one Boldini depicted in his portrait of Montesquiou (fig. 95).[22]

While it seems certain that Whistler worked for some time on a portrait of Montesquiou in day clothes—the "long grey coat" portrait—he and his subject obviously preferred to concentrate on the surviving canvas, in which Montesquiou appears in conventional black evening garb, following the precedent of Whistler's earlier portraits of Leyland (fig. 122), Duret (fig. 115), and Sarasate (fig. 124). Duret recalled just how Whistler had come to paint him as he later would paint Montesquiou:

> From that point on the conversation turned to the dress and pose to choose in a portrait. We [Duret and Whistler] agreed that one should have individuals pose differently, according to their physique, and to dress them in clothes they normally wear. However, the black evening suit, *evening dress,* was a garment in which the English gentlemen spent a good part of their life… and yet no one ever painted anyone wearing it. Was it really so repellent and did it offer such difficulties of execution that artists

115 Whistler, *Arrangement in Flesh Color and Black: Portrait of Théodore Duret,* oil, 1883-84, New York, Metropolitan Museum of Art

should avoid it systematically? The conclusion was to paint "the black evening suit" and, after a moment of reflection, Whistler asked me to pose.…He decided next that it would be full-length, lifesize, with a light background.…After that it was necessary to find…an accessory, something that would make a man in black from head to toe less grim.…Whistler thought for rather a long time [then] said to me: "Come on whatever day, bring your evening suit and a pink cloak for a masquerade." [23]

It was only proper that one of the most successful portraits of Whistler—Nicholson's wood engraving (fig. 116)—should have shown him wearing a similar garment.

Few details of the evening suit in the portrait of Montesquiou are to be discerned, but comparison with 1884 photographs of Montesquiou in evening dress (fig. 117) and with La Gandara's portrait of him from about the same date (fig. 118) suggests that he favored a short, close-fitting jacket with a peaked collar (the upper part of which appears to have been velvet), four buttons on the front, three at the cuff, and two at center back. This jacket had tails that fell to the knees. Sartorio's photographs show the jacket hanging open, revealing a white waistcoat, but in Whistler's portrait the waistcoat is black, of silk, and probably has a collar. The trousers have a pleat at the waist, piping along the side, and no cuffs. No jewelry, such as a watch chain, is apparent, but a flower appears in the buttonhole of the jacket. This type of black worsted evening suit, called a *frac* or *habit,* varied little over the years and appeared to have been worn identically in Paris and London (cf. fig. 119). Montesquiou must have savored the eeriness of this black ensemble, for he inscribed his three Sartorio photographs "*Vespertiliens,*" or "bats."

With this outfit Montesquiou would have worn a heavily starched linen shirt called a *plastron* (breast-plate), with an upstanding collar high under the jaw and a white silk cravat loosely knotted in the "butterfly" style. His shoes, whose narrow pointed tip Whistler highlighted in the portrait with two dashes of grey, would have been ankle-high boots composed of two parts: a japanned leather vamp over the instep and a box-cloth top that buttoned up to the ankle.

Montesquiou's accessories included white gloves, probably of lamb or kid, that, as shown in La Gandara's portrait (fig. 118), had three ribs on the outside. The full cuff was unusual. For one critic of 1894 it conveyed "the entire Charles IX soul of the count," referring to Charles IX (1550–1574), king of France, poet, and tortured soul;[24] for others it recalled Velázquez' portraits of the gloved nobles at the court of Spain (cf. fig. 128).

In this gloved right hand, Montesquiou is shown holding an extremely delicate cane called a *badine.* Its handle is neither the massive gold knob shown in Gerschel's photograph of the count (fig. 114) nor the precious crutch-shaped handle shown in Boldini's portrait (fig. 95). Rather it appears to be a relatively simple, curved handle of a style called "crow's beak." Its coloring suggests it was ivory. Montesquiou's collection of canes was famous. The handles of some were in fact of ivory; others were of gold, or decorated with turquoises, enamels, lapis lazuli, or netsuke. Their provenances too were rich: the cane shown in Boldini's portrait had

116 W. Nicholson, *James McNeill Whistler,* wood engraving, n.d., New York Public Library

belonged to Louis XV and was acquired by Yturri for Montesquiou at the sale of the effects of Edmond de Goncourt.[25]

The extreme fineness of the staff fascinated observers of Whistler's portrait. It recalls the artist's own exaggeratedly long canes, like the one shown in his portrait by Chase (fig. 1). Such staffs would have been made from Malacca, bamboo, blackthorn, or ebony. An observer present at Montesquiou's duel with Henri de Régnier in 1897 described the former carrying a cane that could well have been the one shown in Whistler's portrait:

> This one was a shadow, a puff, a nothing, a gossamer thread, the phantom of a rod, a ghost of a stick! Something so light, so thin, and so delicate, so attenuated! ah!…of a wood so tenderly etiolated and so sveltely flexible that a stem of a poppy would have mastered it rather than have its head cut off.[26]

Absent from Montesquiou's portrait but certainly a crucial element of his wardrobe was a silk top hat like that shown in one of the photographs of the count by Sartorio (fig. 117). With a curved brim and tapering sides, it measured probably about 20 cm. in height. A similar one, in grey silk matching the poet's suit, appears in the right foreground of Boldini's portrait (fig. 95).

The final element of clothing to be discussed in relation to the portrait is the garment shown hanging over Montesquiou's left arm. Described by some as his overcoat, by others as a woman's evening cloak like the one in Whistler's portrait of Duret (fig. 115), it was in fact a chinchilla cape belonging to the poet's beloved muse, the Comtesse Greffulhe. Its presence in the portrait was clearly intended as a subtle reference to their close relationship, one of the few never broken up by this prickly man. It was the countess herself who provided the evidence for identifying this highly important element in Whistler's *Arrangement,* in a conversation with the American literary historian Mina Curtiss:

> I was very fond of Robert and he was devoted to me. But that didn't blind me to his faults. The very last thing he did we none of us could understand. It shocked us very much that he chose to be buried at Versailles next to that thief Yturri instead of in the Merovingian cemetery with his own family. [His parents were in fact buried in the cemetery of Père Lachaise, Paris.] "I didn't know he was a thief," I said. "I thought he was just a counterbounder."…I have good proof of his thievery, she went on. You know Whistler's portrait of Robert. You must have seen it in New York. You know the long cape folded over his arm. Well, that was my chinchilla cape. Robert wanted something of mine to be in the portrait. So because it was light to hold I loaned it to him. About a year or so later when I was sure the portrait must be completed I asked Robert to return my cape. "But, my dear," he said, "you must have forgotten. I gave it to Yturri to bring back to you six months ago."[27]

The countess' tale is partially corroborated by a fragmentary copy of an undated letter Montesquiou sent his cousin which turned up amid other letters from him that she had preserved: "The chinchilla was returned to the rue d'Astorg [8 rue d'Astorg, the Greffulhes' Paris residence] about two years ago."[28]

117 I. Sartorio, *Three Photographs of Montesquiou in Evening Dress,* photocards, 1884, Paris, private collection

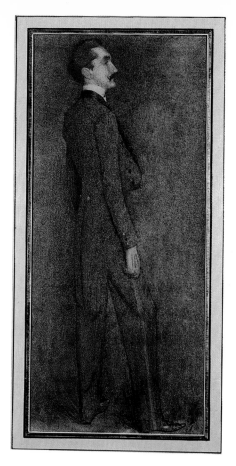

The fur of the chinchilla, a rodent inhabiting the Andes in Chile and Bolivia, being extremely fragile and costly, was usually employed at this time only as trim for women's coats or for muffs, but capes in chinchilla or ermine (cf. fig. 120) were made by fashionable Parisian furriers such as Revillon, just as they are today (fig. 121). The combination of the dusky white and charcoal-grey mottled surface of this fur must have appealed to Whistler independently of the romantic significance of the cape in his portrait.

Montesquiou's concern for his appearance was no doubt carried to the same extremes to which he took every other aspect of his existence, yet basically it was just another characteristic of his class and time, as Thorstein Veblen noted with irony in 1899:

> Much of the charm that invests the patent-leather shoe, the stainless linen, the lustrous cylindrical hat, and the walking stick, which so greatly enhance the native dignity of a gentleman, comes of their pointedly suggesting that the wearer cannot so attired bear a hand in any employment that is directly and immediately of any human use. [29]

119 G. du Maurier, *Terrible Result of the Higher Education of Women,* engraving, from *English Society at Home,* Boston, 1881, New York, Metropolitan Museum of Art

120 Unknown artist, *Highlife,* from *American Album of Fur Novelties,* New York, June 1904, New York, Metropolitan Museum of Art

121 Revillon, Inc., *Chinchilla Cape,* 1993, New York, Revillon, Inc.

The Black
Portraits

Whistler's image of Montesquiou belongs to the genus of the artist's "black" portraits. It was referred to as such by Whistler when he wrote to his wife in January 1892 about "this great black work that still is there—an eternal terror and reproach until it is done," [1] and again when it was exhibited in 1894 as *Noir et or:—Portrait du comte Robert de Montesquiou-Fezensac* (fig. 125).

The artist was employing musical and color titles as early as 1867 with the *Symphony in White, No. 2: The Little White Girl* (London, Tate Gallery), but the first painting to have a "black" title was the portrait of Frederick R. Leyland (fig. 122), catalogued at Whistler's first one-man exhibition in 1874 as *Portrait, Arrangement in Black*. Subsequently, some forty paintings were assigned "black" titles, along with accompanying designations of *Arrangements, Harmonies,* and *Nocturnes*. They included urban views, landscapes, and portraits, of which only a few will be discussed here.

The Leyland portrait, painted between 1870 and 1873, is strikingly similar to Montesquiou's of twenty years later, the major difference being a stronger sense of floor meeting wall in the background of the earlier work. Both show men in black evening clothes, carrying grey garments over their bent left arms, the figures isolated in dark interiors devoid of furniture, hangings, wall treatments, or light source—so unlike the two celebrated *Arrangements in Grey and Black* depicting Carlyle and the artist's mother (fig. 10). The heights of the Leyland and Montesquiou canvases (192.8 and 208.6 cm. respectively) permitted Whistler to represent his subjects standing and life-size. Thomas Way, Jr., corroborated that this was indeed the artist's intention, recalling that "the number of full lengths of life-size which he finished or began and did not complete was very great. I seem to remember that he once explained to me that the full length was the only real way to treat a portrait, so as to give a complete impression of the sitter." [2]

Between 1876 and 1878 Whistler executed his portrait of the artist Rosa Corder (fig. 123), a work that he would refer to alternatively as the fifth and the seventh of his *Arrangements in Black*. According to Jacques-Émile Blanche, the artist conceived the Corder painting after seeing the subject wearing a brown dress pass in front of a black door. Whistler must then have opened such a door, because Corder recalled posing interminably "in a doorway with the darkness of a shuttered room beyond." [3] As with the Leyland portrait, Whistler was again enclosing his subject within a dark restricted space, a sort of *camera obscura*. At least Corder was permitted to turn her gaze away from the viewer who would one day be contemplating her image. Much as Montesquiou would want to adopt the same profile pose, he was not permitted to do so.

It is with Whistler's 1884 portrait of the violinist Pablo de Sarasate y Navascuez, called *Arrangement in Black* (fig. 124), that circumstantial evidence combines with critical interpretation to provide an explanation of what the artist was after in his black portraits and how he went about achieving it. Writing to his subject, he summed up his intentions quite simply: "If my portrait conveys your great artistic air, I shall be quite proud of my work." [4] Whistler, in short, was not concerned primarily with reproducing the musician's physical appearance, though viewers found the portrait to be a good resemblance. Instead, he was seeking to

122 Whistler, *Arrangement in Black: Portrait of F.R. Leyland,* oil, 1871–73, Washington, Freer Gallery of Art

123 Whistler, *Arrangement in Brown and Black: Portrait of Miss Rosa Corder,* oil, 1875–78, New York, Frick Collection

capture and then transmit to others Sarasate's "artistic air," the immaterial part of the man—his soul.

Whistler's success at achieving this was recognized by the critic Alfred de Lostalot, who in 1886 described the portrait as "a sort of apparition of the celebrated violinist called up by some medium in a séance of spiritualism."[5] An unidentified critic writing about the same portrait for the *Magazine of Art* the year before understood the minimalist method of Whistler and described it with rare insight:

> Those not deaf to the language of art will appreciate how, by the means of this simplicity, the unessential details that in real life bury the specialities of men's appearances have been suppressed. In the picture in question only some points are touched firmly and with precision, and these are isolated in a selected emptiness. Thus there is put into open evidence only such things as tell for Mr. Whistler's case—as demonstrated what he feels, and what he intends that those who can read his style shall feel about his sitter. …But then you must take pains to comprehend the *ensemble* and enter into the low tones of the atmosphere of those depths from which Sarasate looks out at you. The gloom is as deep as that of a dark Van Dyck, but blacker, fresher, less mellow; and like that of the Van Dyck, though pitched so low on the scale, it represents air. Therein you will find delicately modelled surfaces of sober colour, immersed as it were in a large, empty, vibrating space, where everything but a rare touch or two is defined as mistily as objects seen through water. Out of this mystery of environment, which suggests much and shows little, the head is revealed, modelled perfectly though imperceptibly, as if by a suffused yet discreet light.…Nothing keeps your eye from the head or unduly diverts your attention from the representation of the man.[6]

To enhance the magical effect of his accomplishment, Whistler would go to elaborate ends to show the portrait in his studio, as the artist Sidney Starr recalled:

> In the Tite Street studio Whistler closed the large door and used a narrow one, three steps up to it. Leaving this door open, he would go down the steps and stand in the passage to look at his work. Through the door, the light coming from the large window on the left, one saw the tall canvas. The portrait finished, one forgot the canvas and became conscious only of…Sarasate…in the late afternoon light. I remember one afternoon he…led me by the arm to the foot of the steps, saying, 'There he is, eh? Isn't that it, eh?.…See how he stands!' It was Sarasate.[7]

From the discussion in a previous chapter of the conditions under which Whistler executed his portrait of Montesquiou, it is apparent that the artist was then following ways he knew to be successful in the past, painting his subject at twilight and without decorative accessories.

Also, Montesquiou's feeling of being "drained" by the artist during the posing sessions was a sensation experienced by many of Whistler's subjects. One writer compared it to the example of an American author often paired with Whistler: "That simple sensation of a being sucked out alive, Edgar Poe described it throughout his short story called "*The*

124 Whistler, *Arrangement in Black:
Portrait of Señor Pablo de Sarasate,* oil,
1884, Pittsburgh, Carnegie Museum
of Art

125 Whistler, *Arrangement in Black
and Gold: Comte Robert de Montesquiou-
Fezensac,* oil, 1891–92, New York,
Frick Collection

157

126 Whistler, *Brown and Gold,* oil,
1895–1900, Glasgow, Hunterian Art
Gallery

127 D. Velázquez, *Gaspar de Guzmán,
Count-Duke of Olivares,* oil, 1625, New
York, Hispanic Society of America

Portrait" [i.e., "The Oval Portrait," 1842, in which a portrait painter literally drains the life from his subject].[8] And another referred to this quality of Whistler's as "the slightly tyrannical taking possession of his models in these portraits with a somber background."[9] The image that resulted from this operation might sometimes be considered by its subject as a disappointing resemblance, as Mallarmé's daughter Geneviève considered hers, but she had to admit, "I sense in it my interior being."[10]

Astute critics at the Salon of 1894, where Montesquiou's portrait was first exhibited (fig. 125), were quick to spot in it the special traits of a Whistler black portrait. Many found the effect magical, as is apparent in the following comments: "[Whistler's subjects] seem to detach themselves bit by bit from the shadow, to come alive."[11] "...the silhouette looms up out of the shadow."[12] "...this apparition...seems to escape from the shadows and come forward toward you."[13] And "...the head shines forth ...much as some evil spirit would appear out of darkness."[14] Whistler's achievement was described as "an art of intense truth"[15] and as "the violent seizing of character,"[16] through which "his portraits are not at all a resemblance to a figure, but a picture of humanity."[17] In the case of Montesquiou's portrait, one critic felt that the artist had captured forever "the lofty and versatile intellect of a nobleman who belongs to another epoch."[18]

This mediumistic interpretation of the black portraits by so many writers reflects the popularity of experiments with the occult at the time. Montesquiou and the Comtesse Greffulhe frequently organized and attended séances at which they sought to see and communicate with the dead, establishing, in Montesquiou's words, "supposed relations between the visible and the invisible."[19] Even as a girl, when asked by her cousin what her feelings were concerning the afterlife, the future countess had replied "an immense curiosity."[20] Montesquiou, on his side, recalled that spiritualism had been the rage in his family from around 1850, his paternal grandfather being a particularly fervent adept who tried to bring the rest of the family around to his philosophy. Even the young man's profound differences with his father were to be resolved for him only by means of a vision he had after Comte Thierry's death. In it, the latter appeared before him asking forgiveness for his "unjust and cruel" behavior, so that he might be spared a "terrible and deserved ordeal [to occur within] thirty-six hours." This dramatic scene concluded with the father's saying to his weeping son, "You give me back good for bad. I bless you again."[21] Finally, though observant of the Catholic faith of his parents, Montesquiou believed with equal fervor in messages he received from the other side, such as this one he reported to Mme Émile Straus: "You are going to learn to know souls."[22]

Whistler too had participated in séances in London in the 1870s and early 1880s, as his friend Alan Cole noted in the following passages from his diaries. On March 12, 1876: "Great conversation on Spiritualism in which Jimmy believes. We tried to get raps—but were unsuccessful except in getting noises from sticky fingers on the table." On April 3, 1878: "Met Jimmy at the Joplings—much talk on spiritualism." On May 13, 1878: "Breakfast with Whistler—Eldon and Lord Lindsay—who related how he had photographed the vibrations caused by spirit raps." And on August 26, 1881: "Jimmy at the Flowers' dinner party talking on the raison

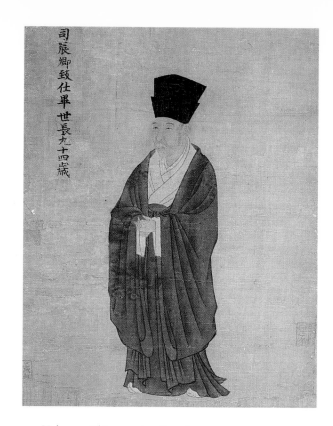

129 Unknown Chinese artist, *Portrait of Pi Shih-ch'ang,* from *Five Old Men of Sui-yang,* ink and color on silk, before 1056, New York, Metropolitan Museum of Art

128 D. Velázquez, *The Infante Don Carlos,* oil, 1626–28, Madrid, Prado

d'etre of artists which was to do *well*—not to do *good*—also on Balzac—magic and spiritualism." [23]

In 1895 the artist finally decided to do a self-portrait in the mode of his other black portraits. His, however, would be half their size (95.8 x 51.5 cm.) and with a dark brown dominant rather than black. The result, *Brown and Gold* (fig. 126), was first exhibited in the American section of the Paris Exposition Universelle of 1900. Gustave Geffroy, who had written so sympathetically of Montesquiou's portrait, saw this one too as through the eyes of a medium, describing it as "vague at first, like an apparition, and so startling, so real." [24] While the pathos of the aged yet somehow cherubic face in this portrait brings to mind Rembrandt's late *Laughing Self-Portrait* (Cologne, Wallraf-Richartz Museum), Whistler's stance and the empty setting recall Velázquez' portrait of the actor *Pablo de Valladolid* (Madrid, Prado), of which Whistler owned a photograph, still preserved at Glasgow. [25]

The mention of the Spanish master's name brings up the other dominant characteristic of the black portraits, along with their magical evocation of the spirit of their subjects, namely, their tendency toward an abstract purity of design connoted by the musical titles *Arrangement, Harmony,* and *Nocturne.* This formal concept so basic to Whistler's art owed a lot to the example of Velázquez, whom the artist deeply admired, though his knowledge of the Spaniard's work was limited. In his earliest days in London and Paris, Whistler could have seen little by the master that would relate to his own later full-lengths, aside from a half-length portrait in the Louvre then thought to depict *Don Pedro Moscoso de Altamira* but now no longer accepted as genuine.[26] Knowing that Velázquez was richly represented in the Art Treasures of the United Kingdom exhibition held at Manchester in the summer of 1857, Whistler went there with Henri Martin and saw the fourteen canvases attributed to his idol. Among them was the portrait of the *Conde Duque de Olivares* (fig. 127), lent by Colonel Hugh Baillie. While not totally devoid of accessories, this portrait possesses a simplicity of design and tonal unity remarkably suggestive of Whistler's later works. In the fall of 1862 Whistler set out with Jo Hiffernan to see the work of Velázquez in Madrid, but got no farther than Guéthary just south of Biarritz, where he was literally swept away painting the raging sea. In later years he could have seen works attributed to Velázquez added to the National Gallery in London, such as the full-length portraits of *Philip IV* and of *Admiral Pulido-Pareja,* purchased in 1882 and 1890.

It was therefore probably from black-and-white reproductions that Whistler came to know the range of Velázquez' work, including his portrait of the *Infante Don Carlos* (fig. 128), of which the artist also owned a photograph.[27] This work along with *Pablo de Valladolid* possessed the essential ingredients Whistler would employ in his black portraits: a somberly dressed figure standing alone in an empty space of a grey-brown tonality, with an invisible light source at lower left provoking a low shadow across the right. From such examples Whistler went on to create his own group of portraits whose character was so succinctly described by Duret, when he wrote of Montesquiou's portrait as follows:

The portrait was designated with the secondary title *Noir et or,* after the arrangement established by the colors. This work is one

130 L. Bonnat, *Portrait of William T. Walters,* oil, 1883, Baltimore, Walters Art Gallery

131 Sir W. Rothenstein, *The Painter
Charles Conder,* oil, 1892, Toledo
Museum of Art

132 P. Helleu, *Portrait of Mme Helleu,* oil,
c. 1904, Paris, private collection

of those in which we can best see how the concern of the artist to obtain combinations of colors takes place without interfering with the rendition of the subject's features. It thus proves that the two qualities, the achievement of beauty through color and the expression of life, can be obtained at the same time and respond one to the other without prejudice.[28]

A totally different and little-noted influence on Whistler's late portraits, and one endowed with spiritualistic overtones, was that of Chinese painting. It was Freer who spoke most authoritatively about this, in a conversation recalled by Louisine Havemeyer:

> "Tell me something about his [Whistler's] art and his work,"
> I asked and Mr. Freer sat thinking a few minutes before he began:
> "Whistler had about given up painting in brilliant colors when I first met him [in March 1890]. I believe it was his appreciation of Oriental paintings that led him to abandon his brilliant palette. He had made a close study of Chinese portraits and was probably actuated by a similar impulse to express the character of his sitter; he tried to have the body only a vehicle for the soul, making his portraits more intense and vital. He ever after sought softer tones and greater harmony, until some of his portraits, like 'Rosa Corder,' are as somber as some of my Chinese monochrome portraits." [29]

Indeed, if one compares a characteristic example of a Chinese portrait (fig. 129) with Whistler's, certain common elements stand out: the muted palette, the figure whose elegant contours are silhouetted against an empty space, the minimum of descriptive detail.

Other artists of the late nineteenth century were experimenting with the portrait in ways remarkably similar to Whistler's, sometimes influenced by his example, sometimes not. A case in point was Léon Bonnat (1834–1923), whose portrait of the American collector *William T. Walters* of 1883 (fig. 130) came so close to those of Whistler in its sparseness. This was, however, but one of many such portraits praised for their "beautiful transparency of shadows" [30] that Bonnat executed from the mid 1870s up into the early years of this century. He had studied in Spain with Federigo Madrazo, so in his case the example of Velázquez' portraits was something experienced firsthand. Later in life, Bonnat would often send friends off to Madrid with a detailed itinerary to follow amid the works of the master in the Prado.

Perhaps the most startling variation on the common theme was the portrait painted by the twenty-one-year-old William Rothenstein (1872–1945) depicting his fellow artist Charles Edward Conder (1868–1909), exhibited in 1893 with the title *L'Homme qui sort* ("The Man who is going out")(fig. 131). While preserving the essential components of the Whistlerian black full-length, Rothenstein had the audacity to turn his figure, spin him around, and confer a cinematic quality to the image. It has been conjectured that the artist was working from a snapshot,[31] but Rothenstein had only this to say of the portrait:

> I was…painting Conder in his studio, in a long overcoat and tall hat….Conder wished me to make him look more *Daumieresque*, to stylise his coat and give him a *fatale* and romantic appearance. He was a born stylist; I was by nature a realist, and I already felt

133 A. Reinhardt, *No. 18,* oil, 1956, New York, private collection

dimly that style should be intrinsic in one's work, not a thing imposed. I painted other and similar full-length figures.[32] Rothenstein knew Whistler at this time and mentioned him frequently in his memoirs, but never in reference to this portrait of Conder.

Finally, even Helleu experimented with the monochromatic portrait genre, most notably in a mauve arrangement depicting his wife, painted around 1904 (fig. 132). Though he most often worked with a light palette and within interiors noted for their white and silver tones, this artist occasionally indulged in darker tonalities, as here where the glow of the gilt-bronze meridian around the eighteenth-century celestial globe shown in the corner sets off the orchidaceous harmonies in a magical way. The artist's daughter Paulette recalled that Whistler had wanted to paint the beautiful Mme Helleu, but her husband had not encouraged the idea.

While there were always those who would say, as did one critic of Whistler's black portraits, that "a vast sheet of black paint must always remain *per se* undecorative and unlovely," [33] more perceptive contemporaries saw them as the natural conclusion of a lifetime spent balancing pure form with representation. Kenyon Cox (1856–1919), an American artist of conservative training and outlook, described Whistler's attainment of "absolute painting" in a remarkably farseeing article published in 1904. Among other points he made the following:

> *His* art…tended less and less to any concern with subject or any immediate connection with nature. It became, as nearly as possible, what one may call "absolute painting" after the analogy of absolute music.… Painting, in his hands, was trying to disassociate itself altogether from representation.…His early pictures are Whistlerian arrangements plus representation; his later are nearly pure arrangements, with representation reduced to a vestige. A step further and we should have line and color entirely for their own sake, with no representative value whatever. Should the step be taken the result might, conceivably, be exquisitely beautiful, but it would be something else than what the world has hitherto known as the art of painting.[34]

Of course the step that Cox envisioned was taken, and not long afterwards. It has been taken again and again throughout the twentieth century, and when one contemplates today the results achieved—to cite a sole example, by Ad Reinhardt (1913-67) (fig. 133)—the debt to Whistler is enormous.

Bibliography of Works Cited in Abbreviated Form

Barbier. C. P. Barbier (ed.), *Correspondance Mallarmé—Whistler*, Paris, 1964

Duret. T. Duret, *Histoire de J. McN. Whistler et de son oeuvre*, Paris, 1904

Eddy. A. J. Eddy, *Recollections and Impressions of James A. McNeill Whistler*, Philadelphia—London, 1903

Glasgow. Whistler Archives, Department of Special Collections, Glasgow University Library

Goncourt. J. and E. de Goncourt, *Journal—Mémoires de la vie littéraire*, ed. R. Ricatte, Paris, 1989

Havemeyer. L. Havemeyer, *From Sixteen to Sixty, Memoirs of a Collector*, New York, 1961

Jullian. P. Jullian, *Robert de Montesquiou, un prince 1900*, Paris, 1965

Lavery. Sir J. Lavery, *The Life of a Painter*, London, 1940

Levy. M. Levy, *Whistler's Lithographs, An Illustrated Catalogue Raisonné*, London, 1975

Montesquiou, *Altesses*. R. de Montesquiou, *Altesses sérénissimes*, Paris, 1907

Montesquiou, *Assemblée*. R. de Montesquiou, *Assemblée de notables*, Paris, 1908

Montesquiou, *Autels*. R. de Montesquiou, *Autels privilégiés*, Paris, 1898

Montesquiou, *Diptyque*. R. de Montesquiou, *Diptyque de Flandre, Triptyque de France*, Paris, 1921

Montesquiou, *Élus*. R. de Montesquiou, *Élus et appelés, études et essais*, Paris, 1921

Montesquiou, *Hortensias*. R. de Montesquiou, *Les Hortensias bleus*, Paris, 1896

Montesquiou, *Pas*. R. de Montesquiou, *Les Pas effacés, mémoires*, Paris, 1923

Montesquiou, *Professionnelles*. R. de Montesquiou, *Professionnelles beautés*, Paris, 1905

Montesquiou, *Roseaux*. R. de Montesquiou, *Roseaux pensants*, Paris, 1897

Montesquiou, *Têtes*. R. de Montesquiou, *Têtes d'expression*, Paris, 1912

Munhall. E. Munhall, "Whistler's Portrait of Robert de Montesquiou," *Gazette des Beaux-Arts*, April 1968, pp. 231–42

NAF. Nouvelles Acquisitions françaises (1958–71), 15012-15380, Papiers de Robert de Montesquiou, Département des Manuscrits, Bibliothèque Nationale de France, Paris

Newton. J. Newton (ed.), *La Chauve-souris et le papillon, Correspondance Montesquiou-Whistler*, Glasgow, 1990

Pennell. E. R. and J. Pennell, *The Life of James McNeill Whistler*, Philadelphia, 1908

Robertson, *Life*. G. Robertson, *Life Was Worth Living*, New York—London, 1931

Robertson, *Time*. G. Robertson, *Time Was*, London, 1931

Way, 1912. T. R. Way, *Memories of James McNeill Whistler, The Artist*, London, 1912

Way, 1914. T. R. Way, *The Lithographs of Whistler*, ed. E. G. Kennedy, New York, 1914

Young, MacDonald, and Spencer. A. McLaren Young, M. MacDonald, R. Spencer, *The Paintings of James McNeill Whistler*, New Haven—London, 1980

Notes

Introduction

1. Montesquiou, NAF 15288, f. 73.

Whistler First

1. In Young, MacDonald, and Spencer, text vol., pp. lvii–lxxi.
2. J. R. Key, "Recollections of Whistler while in the Office of the United States Coast Survey," *The Century Magazine,* April 1908, p. 932.
3. See M. F. MacDonald, "Maud Franklin," *James McNeill Whistler, a Re-examination, Studies in the History of Art,* XIX, Washington, 1987, pp. 13–26.
4. Key, *loc. cit.*
5. Havemeyer, p. 206.
6. Robertson, *Time,* p. 189.
7. L. Daudet, *Souvenirs littéraires,* Paris, 1968, p. 351.
8. A. Symons, in *Whistler, A Retrospective,* ed. R. Spencer, New York, 1989, p. 348.
9. Lavery, p. 116.
10. W. Gay, *Memoirs of Walter Gay,* New York, 1930, p. 46.

Montesquiou

1. Montesquiou, *Pas,* II, p. 16.
2. *Idem,* p. 62.
3. *Idem,* II, p. 159.
4. The genealogical material above is taken from H. Jougla de Morenas, *Grand Armorial de France,* Paris, 1938, V, pp. 92–93, and A. de Montesquiou, *La Maison de Montesquiou-Fezensac depuis la fin de l'Ancien Régime,* Paris, 1962, pp. 62–64, 162–66.
5. Montesquiou, *Pas,* I, p. 202.
6. *Idem,* pp. 210, 203.
7. *Idem,* p. 218.
8. *Idem,* p. 339.
9. *Idem,* p. 349.
10. *Idem,* p. 354.
11. Montesquiou, *Hortensias,* p. 352.
12. Montesquiou, *Pas,* II, p. 53.
13. *Idem,* p. 83.
14. Goncourt, III, p. 782.
15. Montesquiou, *Pas,* I, p. 91.
16. *Idem,* p. 97.
17. *Idem,* p. 115.
18. NAF 15037, fs. 124–33. For published examples, see P. Jullian, "Ce que l'art nouveau doit à la curiosité fantasque de Robert de Montesquiou," *Connaissance des Arts,* July 1965, p. 63, and N. Reymond, "Robert de Montesquiou et l'art de son temps," *Information d'histoire de l'art,* numéro 1, 1973, p. 21, figs. 2, 3.
19. Robertson, *Life,* p. 100.
20. Montesquiou, *Pas,* II, p. 123.
21. Goncourt, III, p. 605.
22. On the symbolism of the bat, see M. B. Fenton, *Bats,* New York, 1992, pp. 179–87, and J. Chevalier, *Dictionnaire des symboles,* Paris, 1982, pp. 172–73.
23. Montesquiou, *Pas,* II, p. 303.
24. *Idem,* pp. 103, 104, 105.
25. Newton 53.
26. Montesquiou, *Pas,* II, p. 205.
27. *Idem,* p. 206.
28. Goncourt, III, p. 604. The photograph in question, identified as representing "*X...de La Rochefoucauld, gymnaste au cirque Molier*" (i.e., Hubert de la Rochefoucauld [1855–1936]), has been preserved among Montesquiou's papers at the Bibliothèque Nationale de France (NAF 15038, f. 73). The phenomenon of aristocrats performing as amateurs at the Cirque Molier was the subject of James Tissot's painting *Les Femmes de Sport* of 1883–85 (Boston Museum of Fine Arts).
29. Unidentified newspaper clipping dated March 12, 1893, NAF 15039, f. 47.
30. Montesquiou, *Le Chancelier de fleurs,* Paris, 1907, p. 34.
31. *Idem,* p. 44.
32. *Idem,* pp. 138, 139.
33. *Idem,* p. 59.
34. *Idem,* p. 298.
35. Montesquiou, *Hortensias,* p. ix.
36. Newton 97.
37. F. Bac, *Intimités de la IIIè République, La Fin des "Temps délicieux," Souvenirs Parisiens,* Paris, 1935, pp. 187–88.
38. E. de Clermont-Tonnerre, *Robert de Montesquiou et Marcel Proust,* Paris, 1925, pp. 55–56.
39. L. Daudet, *Souvenirs et polémiques,* Paris, 1992, p. 303.
40. Montesquiou, *Pas,* II, p. 133.
41. See P. Apraxine *et al., The Waking Dream, Photography's First Century,* exhib. cat., New York, 1993, p. 339.
42. Montesquiou, *La Divine Comtesse, Étude d'après Madame de Castiglione,* Paris, 1913, pp. 16–17.
43. A. de Cossé-Brissac, *La Comtesse Greffulhe,* Paris, 1991, p. 76.
44. Montesquiou, *La Divine Comtesse,* pp. 202–03.
45. *Idem,* p. 205.
46. Montesquiou, *Pas,* II, p. 149.
47. *Idem,* p. 283.
48. Goncourt, III, p. 905.

49. Unidentified newspaper clipping, NAF 15047, f. 29.

50. L. Marsoleau, "En passant," *Le Rappel,* NAF 15047, f. 52.

51. In E. Cardona, *Vie de Jean Boldini,* Paris, 1931, p. 86.

52. Montesquiou, *Pas,* III, p. 12.

53. *Idem,* p. 61.

54. *Idem,* pp. 62–63.

55. *Idem,* p. 63.

56. Montesquiou, "Le Pavillon des Muses," *La Revue contemporaine,* July 25, 1901, p. 162.

57. Newspaper clipping from *La Liberté,* dated February 25, 1901, NAF 15049, f. 81.

58. The incident is discussed in Montesquiou, *Pas,* III, pp. 114–15.

59. "Les Départs," clipping from an unidentified journal dated November 1902, NAF 15053, f. 23.

60. E. Marbury, *My Crystal Ball, Reminiscences,* New York, 1923, p. 120.

61. J. Montague, "Beautiful Count Talks to Society Women," *New York Evening Journal,* February 6, 1903.

62. Montesquiou, "Le Mystère," NAF 15056, f. 11.

63. *Le Figaro,* January 18, 1904, NAF 15063, f. 25.

64. NAF 15063, f. 94.

65. Montesquiou, *Chancelier,* p. 15.

66. *Idem,* p. 28.

67. A. Alexandre, "Opinions, Étude de moeurs," *Le Figaro,* undated clipping, NAF 15040, f. 213.

68. P. Morand, *1900,* Paris, 1931, pp. 232–33.

69. *The Letters of Bernard Berenson and Isabella Stewart Gardner, 1887–1924,* ed. R. Hadley, Boston, 1988, p. 345.

70. A. H. Mayor, "A. Hyatt Mayor Abroad," *Archives of American Art Journal,* XXXII, no. 4, 1992, pp. 15–16.

71. M. Proust, *Lettres à Robert de Montesquiou,* ed. R. Proust and P. Brach, Paris, 1930, pp. 282, 284.

72. Montesquiou, *Pas,* II, pp. 284, 286.

73. *Idem,* III, p. 229.

74. *Idem.*

75. Letter dated April 25, 1921, NAF 15093, f. 147.

76. Letter dated "Pâques 1921," NAF 15093, f. 108.

77. Letter dated March 24, 1921, NAF 15093, f. 79.

78. Letter dated April 30, 1921, NAF 15093, ff. 6–7.

79. NAF 15093, f. 251.

80. I am grateful to Vicomte Jacques d'Arjuzon for having obtained a copy of this document for me from the civil records of the city of Menton.

81. *Le Petit Journal,* December 22, 1921, NAF 15093, f. 272.

82. Unidentified clipping from *Le Figaro* dated December 22, 1921, NAF 15093, f. 271.

83. In *L'Écho de Versailles,* December 22, 1921, NAF 15093, f. 265.

84. L. Delarue-Mardrus, "Hommage au poète Robert de Montesquiou," *Le Journal,* February 7, 1921, NAF 15093, f. 283.

85. L. Corpechet, "Le Comte Robert de Montesquiou," *Le Gaulois,* December 15, 1921, NAF 15093, f. 253.

The Evolution of the Portrait

1. NAF 15335, f. 81.

2. Manuscript Division, Houghton Library, Harvard University, Cambridge (b MS AM 1094 [396]), quoted by T. F. Fairbrother in *A New World: Masterpieces of American Painting, 1760–1910,* ed. J. G. Silver, exhib. cat., Boston, 1983, p. 300, n. 1. I am grateful to Nigel Thorp for directing me to this letter.

3. Paris, private collection.

4. Newton 1. Newton transcribed the salutation as "*Chers Messieurs*"; I read it as "*Cher Monsieur.*"

5. Quoted in D. M. Murray, "James and Whistler at the Grosvenor Gallery," *American Quarterly,* Spring 1952, p. 56.

6. Montesquiou, *Pas,* II, p. 243–44.

7. NAF 15335, f. 52.

8. Quoted in Jullian, pp. 128–29.

9. L. Edel, *Henry James: The Middle Years,* Philadelphia [1962], p. 150.

10. Newton 2.

11. Newton 3.

12. Newton 4.

13. Newton 6–8.

14. Newton 10.

15. Newton 13.

16. Newton 15.

17. Newton 16.

18. Newton 22. Whistler would eventually receive the miniature tree in January 1890 (see Newton 29).

19. Newton 24.

20. Newton 25.

21. See Newton 23.

22. Newton 34.

23. Newton 39.

24. Newton 40.

25. Paris, private collection. I am grateful to Joy Newton for helping me decipher and translate this letter.

26. Newton 41.

27. In my article "Whistler's Portrait of Robert de Montesquiou: The Documents," *Gazette des Beaux-Arts,* April 1968, pp. 231–42, I suggested (p. 232) that Whistler did not begin work on the portrait until November 1891. However, Newton's letters 40–48 (of which any undated ones from Montesquiou were dated by himself when he turned his letters over to Rosalind Birnie Philip in 1908), make it clear that work had begun in the spring of 1891. For some reason I had not seen those letters at the time I wrote my article.

28. Newton 43.

29. Newton 42.

30. Robertson, *Life,* p. 257.

31. Newton 44.

32. Newton 47. See also Young, MacDonald, and Spencer, text vol., No. 397.

33. Goncourt, III, pp. 604–05. On Montesquiou's relations with Edmond de Goncourt, see J. Newton and M. Fol, "Robert de Montesquiou et Edmond de Goncourt: Une Amitié littéraire," *Nineteenth-Century French Studies,* VII, 1978–79, pp. 85–103.

34. Quoted in Barbier, p. 129.

35. Young, MacDonald, and Spencer, text vol., No. 397; Newton 119. The X-ray examination was carried out under Dr. Hubert von Sonnenburg's supervision on February 28, 1994.

36. Newton 48.

37. Eddy, pp. 242, 234. On Grau, see I. M. Horowitz, "Whistler's Frames," *Art Journal,* Winter 1979–80, p. 131.

38. Newton 53.

39. Newton 55.

40. Newton 59.

41. Newton 63.

42. Newton 64.

43. Newton, pp. 128, 130. Newton has analyzed the poem with admirable thoroughness (pp. 124-33).

44. Montesquiou, *Pas,* II, p. 262.

45. *Idem,* p. 259.

46. *Idem,* p. 245.

47. Interview with the author, September 26, 1993. Eddy (p. 119) also commented on Whistler's way of speaking: "Whistler had a very peculiar laugh, demoniacal his enemies called it, and it is said that while his portrait was being painted, Irving caught this laugh and

used it with effect in the part of Mephistopheles, but then, who knows?"

48. Montesquiou, *Pas*, II, pp. 259–62.

49. Eddy, pp. 235–36.

50. Newton 66.

51. In Barbier, p. 124.

52. Newton 67.

53. Newton 68.

54. In M. F. MacInnes, "Whistler's Last Years," *Gazette des Beaux-Arts*, May-June 1969, p. 330.

55. Newton 69.

56. I am grateful to Madeleine Fidell-Beaufort for supplying much of this information (letter of November 8, 1993). See also J. Milner, *The Studios of Paris*, New Haven—London, 1988, p. 207.

57. Newton 74.

58. Newton 79.

59. Newton 75.

60. Montesquiou, *Professionnelles*, p. 120. I am grateful to Margaret MacDonald for informing me that Whistler's original table palette is in the Tate Gallery, London.

61. Eddy, p. 231.

62. Newton 80.

63. Quoted in Young, MacDonald, and Spencer, text vol., No. 402, p. 180; unknown critic, *The Times*, London, May 20, 1894 (NAF 15288, f. 126).

64. Newton 70.

65. Newton 75.

66. Newton 76.

67. Newton 78.

68. Newton 84.

69. L. Pearsall Smith, *Unforgotten Years*, Boston, 1939, pp. 206–09.

70. Newton 82.

71. Newton 83.

72. Newton 81.

73. Quoted in Eddy, p. 214.

74. *Idem*, pp. 213–14.

75. NAF 15288, f. 98.

76. Newton 90.

77. "A Gossip at Goupil's. Mr. Whistler on His Works," *The Illustrated London News*, March 26, 1892, p. 384.

78. Newton 75.

79. Milner, p. 211.

80. In Eddy, p. 229.

81. Information kindly provided by Hortense Damiron.

82. Eddy, pp. 131, 134.

83. In Barbier, p. 162.

84. Newton 102.

85. See: M. Praz, *On Neoclassicism*, London, 1969, pp. 178, 307; Montesquiou, *Pas*, I, pp. 160-61.

86. H. Jougla de Morenas, *Grand Armorial de France*, Paris, 1938, V, p. 92;

Montesquiou, *Pas*, I, pp. 160–61.

87. Newton 103. In addition to this version of the letter preserved at Glasgow, another, probably a draft, belongs to The Frick Collection (acc. no. 72.12.3). It is identical in every respect, except for the incorrect spelling "*efrenée*" in the reference to "unbridled passion."

88. Newton 105.

89. Newton 106.

90. Newton 104.

91. Munhall, 1968, p. 238.

92. A. Bertrand, "Robert de Montesquiou et l'Abbaye de Créteil," *Revue de la Bibliothèque Nationale*, No. 26, Winter 1987, pp. 12–34.

93. E. de Clermont-Tonnerre, *Robert de Montesquiou et Marcel Proust*, Paris, 1925, pp. 56–57.

94. Eddy, p. 272.

95. Saint-Charles, "Un Tableau de Whistler," *Le Figaro*, November 27, 1891, quoted in Barbier, p. 128, n. 2.

96. See: S. Houfe, "David Croal Thomson, Whistler's 'Aide-de-Camp,'" *Apollo*, February 1984, pp. 117–18; M. F. MacDonald, "The Selling of Whistler's 'Mother,'" *The American Society of The Legion of Honor Magazine*, XLIX, No. 2, 1978, pp. 100, 104, 106; Young, MacDonald, and Spencer, text vol., Nos. 408, 402, 425, 315, 481, 547, 550.

97. Information on the value of the pound kindly provided by Patrick Cooney of The Citibank Private Bank, New York, and Richard Jackman of The London School of Economics and Political Science. Dennis Collins kindly supplied similar information for the franc.

98. Goncourt, III, p. 709.

99. In *Gil Blas*, May 5, 1895; quoted in Munhall, 1968, p. 237.

100. Newton 124.

101. Newton 107.

102. Newton 109.

103. Newton 110.

104. Eddy, pp. 262–63, 272.

105. Newton 119. The telegram must date from mid March 1894, for the official catalogue of the exhibition stated, under Article 2 of its rules: "The artists must send their works to the Champ de Mars between March 18 and 22." In Société Nationale des Beaux-Arts, *Catalogue des ouvrages de peinture, sculpture, dessin, gravure, architecture et objets d'art exposés au Champ-de-Mars le 25 avril 1894*, Paris, 1894, p. 303.

The Salon of 1894, and Beyond

1. The iron fittings for the pulley are still in place over the window of the studio.

2. E. Hoschedé, *Brelan de Salons*, Paris, 1890, p. xi.

3. "Art and Mr. Whistler," *Art Journal*, II, 1894, p. 360.

4. Goncourt, III, pp. 949–50.

5. *Correspondance de Camille Pissarro*, ed. J. Bailly-Herzberg, Paris, 1988, III, p. 446.

6. Robertson, *Time*, pp. 236–37.

7. *Letters from Graham Robertson*, ed. K. Preston, London, 1953, pp. 367, 368.

8. Lavery, p. 89.

9. *Idem*, p. 92; quoted in K. McConkey, *Sir John Lavery, R. A., 1856–1941*, Edinburgh, 1984, p. 43.

10. Lavery, p. 89; quoted in McConkey, *loc. cit.*

11. *The Studio*, May 1, 1894, NAF 15288, f. 125.

12. *Le Siècle*, April 24, 1894, NAF 15288, f. 122 ; *The Times*, May 20, 1894, NAF 15288, f. 126.

13. R. Milès, *Le Salon de 1894*, Paris, 1894, pp. 71–72, 73.

14. *Paris-Mode*, May 13, 1894, NAF 15288, f. 126.

15. *The Builder*, June 2, 1894, NAF 15288, f. 128.

16. *Paris*, April 24, 1894, NAF 15288, f. 122.

17. *Le XIXème Siècle*, April 25, 1894, NAF 15288, f. 123.

18. *The Nineteenth Century*, June 1, 1894, NAF 15288, f. 128.

19. G. Geffroy, *La Justice*, April 25, 1894, NAF 15288, f. 123.

20. *Le Temps*, April 27, 1894, NAF 15288, f. 124.

21. *Le Journal*, April 24, 1894, NAF 15288, f. 122.

22. NAF 15288, f. 125. An unsigned and untitled article in *L'Évènement* on July 13, 1895 (NAF 15335, f. 11), provided the identity of the caricaturist who produced *Le Hareng saur*: "The year in which the star of Monsieur Robert de Montesquiou-Fezensac rose above our foreheads, upset that onerous duties had prevented me from admiring at the Salon of the Champ-de-Mars the painting that Whistler had devoted to him, I asked—in vain, alas!—for a photograph of it at the stationers. Having never seen this astonishing poet, this singer of bats and glorifier of hydrangeas, I was obliged, to familiarize myself with his type of physical beauty or at least to imagine it,

to be satisfied with the caricaturistic fantasy in an illustrated paper, with which the draughtsman Albert Guillaume pretended to counterfeit by synthesis Whistler's portrait with the species of a smoked herring hanging on display: in painting or in literature, Guillaume is not the first to have produced a grocer's article."

23. NAF 15040, f. 8. I am grateful to Daniel Meyer for the information he provided on Montesquiou's residences at Versailles, citing E. and M. Houth, *Versailles aux trois visages,* Versailles, 1980, pp. 656-57.

24. *Le Journal,* May 31, 1894, NAF 15040, f. 122.

25. J. Saint-Cère, "Une Heure chez le Comte Robert de Montesquiou," *La Revue illustrée,* August 1, 1894, pp. 18-19.

26. R. de Montesquiou, "Le Pavillon des Muses," *La Revue contemporaine,* July 25, 1901, pp. 157-58.

27. É. Berr, "Le Pavillon des Muses," *Le Figaro,* June 21, 1901

28. I. d'Arcy Morell, "American Tour of Comte de Montesquiou," *Paris World,* February 1903 (NAF 15053, f. 30).

29. Newton 120.

30. Newton 121.

31. Newton 122.

32. Newton 123.

33. In A. Gardiner, *Richard Albert Canfield (1855–1914): The True Story of the Greatest Gambler,* New York, 1930, p. 235.

34. Letter from Canfield to Whistler dated October 22, 1902 (Glasgow, Whistler C30).

35. Glasgow, C 31. Quoted in Newton, p. 228.

36. Letter from Canfield to Whistler dated December 17, 1902 (Glasgow, Whistler C 34).

37. Glasgow, C 32.

38. Glasgow, C 33.

39. Newton 124. "Rue Lafitte" refers to the alternative address of Montesquiou's Neuilly residence, located at the corner of the boulevard Maillot and the rue Charles Laffitte.

40. Newton 125.

41. E. R. and J. Pennell, *The Whistler Journal,* Philadelphia, 1921, p. 270.

42. NAF 15050, f. 13.

43. *La Bavarde,* November 10, 1902.

44. Glasgow, Whistler X 51–54.

45. *Idem.*

46. Glasgow, V 74.

47. *Idem.*

48. Glasgow, X 51–54.

49. Glasgow, V 73.

50. F. Bac, *Intimités de la IIIᵉ République, La Fin des "Temps délicieux," Souvenirs parisiens,* Paris, 1935, p. 173.

51. NAF 15335, f. 88.

52. Glasgow, LB6, pp. 4, 6. I am grateful to Nigel Thorp for supplying me with a copy of this letter.

53. G. H. Kennedy, Jr., "A Gambler's Gift to Art," *New York Herald Tribune,* February 12, 1933, p. 9.

54. *Idem,* p. 10.

55. Gardiner, p. 150.

56. Kennedy, p. 10.

57. "My dear Mr. Carstairs: A propos of our talk today, I am sending you a catalogue of my collection of Whistler's art…." Letter preserved in the archives of M. Knoedler and Co., New York. The catalogue mentioned is also in the Knoedler archives.

58. Record Book No. 6, *Invoices/Paintings/Dec. 1911/Dec. 1920,* p. 87, No. 13428, Knoedler archives. I am grateful to Melissa Madeiros for guiding me through the Knoedler records.

59. *Idem.*

60. *Paintings and Other Works of Art Owned by Henry C. Frick,* p. 126, No. 214, preserved in The Frick Collection archives.

61. Letter from Robert Clark to Stephen Clark preserved in the archives of the Sterling and Francine Clark Art Institute, Williamstown, Massachusetts. I am grateful to David Brooke for bringing this letter to my attention.

62. Pennell, p. 271.

63. "The Art Galleries/Fifth Avenue's New Museum," *New Yorker,* December 28, 1935.

64. "Frick Museum Finally Opened to the Public," *New York Sun,* December 11, 1935.

65. E. C. Sherburne, "The Frick Collection," *Christian Science Monitor,* February 12, 1936, p. 9.

66. E. A. Jewell, "In the Realm of Art: The Frick Collection Opens," *New York Times,* December 15, 1935.

67. J. J. Cowan, *From 1846 to 1932,* Edinburgh, 1933, p. 157.

68. The conservation reports quoted above are preserved in the The Frick Collection archives.

The Lithographs

1. *Pall Mall Budget,* No. 1176, April 9, 1891, reproduced full-page on the cover. See Young, MacDonald, and Spencer, text vol., No. 137.

2. Washington, Library of Congress, Whistler collection, Container 3, Folder "Thomson D. Croal," March-July 1894. The letter referred to in Whistler's postscript, which Thomson sent on April 27 (Glasgow, T 151), mentioned only "a small illustration for the Art Journal" and an opportunity to have the portrait reproduced in the *Figaro Salon.* Ultimately, Montesquiou's portrait was not reproduced in the 1894 issue of the latter, nor was it even mentioned by Yriarte in his description of the Champ-de-Mars exhibition. Charles Brock kindly supplied copies of relevant letters from Whistler to Thomson preserved at the Library of Congress.

3. Library of Congress, Whistler collection, Container 3.

4. Glasgow, T 156.

5. "Art and Mr. Whistler," *The Art Journal,* 1894, pp. 358, 360.

6. Library of Congress, Whistler collection, Container 3.

7. Claudie Bertin discusses the Guérard print in her forthcoming catalogue raisonné of that artist's work (No. 548). Information kindly communicated by her and Claude Bouret.

8. Washington, Freer Gallery of Art, Letter File, Folder 126. Copies of relevant letters from Whistler to Way were kindly supplied by Nesta Spink.

9. Freer Gallery of Art, Letter File, Folder 127.

10. *Idem,* Folder 129.

11. *Idem,* Folder 125.

12. *Idem,* Folder 130.

13. *Idem,* Folder 137a.

14. Way, 1912, pp. 106–07.

15. The standard references for this print and other lithographs by Whistler are: Way, 1914, No. 107; Levy, No. 155; and N. Spink, *The Lithographs of James McNeill Whistler,* to be published by The Art Institute of Chicago in 1997. Nesta Spink was most generous in sharing her knowledge of Whistler's lithographs with the author, to the extent of providing him with copies of draft entries for her future catalogue and correcting his first version of the present text. For Whistler's portrait of the elder Way, see also Way, 1912, p. 124.

16. P. Forthuny, "Notes sur James Whistler," *Gazette des Beaux-Arts,* November 1903, facing p. 390.

17. Duret, facing p. 174.

18. T. de Wyzewa, "Le Salon de 1894," *Gazette des Beaux-Arts,* June 1894, p. 468.

19. Way, No. 137; Levy, No. 138; Spink, to be numbered. See also N. Smale, "Whistler and Transfer Lithography," *The Tamarind Papers,* VII, No. 2, 1984, p. 80.

20. Smale, p. 76.

21. Way, No. 138; Levy, No. 133; Spink, to be numbered.

22. Way, No. 139, and Levy, No. 132, both mistakenly dating the print to 1895; M. F. MacDonald, "Whistler's Lithographs," *Print Quarterly,* V, No. 1, March 1988, p. 30; Spink, to be numbered.

23. Way, 1912, p. 91.

24. Not recorded by Way; Levy, No. 134; MacDonald, 1988, p. 30; Spink, to be numbered.

25. Glasgow, A. 85. Nesta Spink brought this letter to the author's attention.

26. Letter dated March 3, 1903 (NAF 15053, f. 123).

The Art Interpreter

1. Montesquiou, *Pas,* II, p. 237.

2. *Idem,* p. 71.

3. *Idem.*

4. *Idem,* p. 89.

5. *Idem.*

6. I am grateful to Catherine Fehrer for checking these archives in quest of Montesquiou. See her *The Julian Academy, Paris 1868–1939,* exhib. cat., New York, Shepherd Gallery, 1989.

7. *Pas,* III, pp. 198–99.

8. A. Alexandre, "Les Aquarelles du poète," *Exposition d'aquarelles et de dessins de feu Robert de Montesquiou,* exhib. cat., Paris, Galeries Georges Petit, 1923, p. 10.

9. A summary listing of references in Montesquiou's writings to the artists mentioned above would include: for Bakst, in *Têtes;* for Beardsley, "Le Pervers," in *Professionnelles,* and "Beardsley en raccourci," in *Assemblées;* for Besnard, "L'Enchanteur," in *Altesses;* for Blake, "Le Voyant," in *Autels;* for Boecklin, "Arnold Boecklin," *La Nouvelle Revue,* December 1, 1897, and "Un Mythologue," in *Autels;* for Boldini, "Le Séducteur," in *Altesses;* for Bresdin, *L'Inextricable Graveur. Rodolphe Bresdin,* Paris, 1913; for Breslau, "Un Maître femme," in *Professionnelles;* for Burne-Jones, "Burne-Jones," *La Revue illustrée,* October 1, 1894, and "Le Spectre," in *Autels;* for Carriès, "Jean Carriès," *Gazette des Beaux-Arts,* September 1894, and "Le Potier," in *Autels;* for Chassériau, "Alice et Aline," in *Autels;* for Gallé, "Les Verres forgés, Exposition d'Émile Gallé au Musée Galliéra," *Les Arts,* October 1910; for Grandville, "Le Buffon de l'Humanité," in *Roseaux;* for Guys, "Fragments sur Constantin Guys," *Le Gaulois,* April 18, 1895; for Helleu, "Un Féministe," in *Autels,* "La Femme par Helleu," *Figaro illustré,* October 1899, "Les Peintres de la femme," *Les Modes,* August 1901, and *Paul Helleu, peintre et graveur,* Paris, 1913; for Ingres, "Le Sphinx," in *Roseaux,* and "Ingres verrier," in *L'Art décoratif,* May 1911, pp. 253–68; for Jacquet, *Catalogue des tableaux, aquarelles, pastels, dessins par Gustave Jacquet,* Paris, 1909; for Lalique, "Le Mobilier libre, orfèvre et verrier," in *Roseaux;* for László, "Philippe Laszlo, un portraitiste lyrique," *L'Art et les artistes,* June 1906, and *Selections from the Work of P.A. de László,* London, 1922; for Lemaire, "L'Impératrice des roses," in *Professionnelles;* for Leonardo, "Le Grand Oiseau," in *Autels;* for Monticelli, "Monticelli," *Gazette des Beaux-Arts,* February 1901; for Moreau, "Un Peintre lapidaire, Gustave Moreau," in *Exposition Gustave Moreau,* exhib. cat., Paris, 1906, and "Le Lapidaire et le refuge des dieux," in *Altesses;* for Rodin, "L'Animateur," in *Altesses;* for Rouveyre, *La Comédie française, album par Rouveyre,* Paris, 1905; for Sargent, "Le Pavé rouge, Quelques Réflexions sur 'l'Oeuvre' de M. Sargent," *Les Arts de la vie,* June 3, 1905; for Stevens, "Alfred Stevens," *Gazette des Beaux-Arts,* February 1900, and "Le Peintre aux billets, Alfred Stevens," in *Diptyque;* for Tissot, "Tissot chrétien," *La Revue illustrée,* May 1896; for Troubetzkoy, "Lettre ouverte au prince Troubetzkoy," in *Altesses,* and *Pas,* III, pp. 83–90; for Vernet, "Les Trois Vernet," *Gazette des Beaux-Arts,* July 1898; for Watteau, "Watteau belligérant," in *Élus;* and for Whistler, in *Pas,* II, pp. 243–62, and "Sur Whistler," *Revue de Genève,* April 1923. Montesquiou's attitudes toward contemporary artists were the subject of a thesis submitted to the Université de Paris I by Mme Mares-Reymond in 1971 and the focus of an article by Jean Pierrot, "Robert de Montesquiou, critique d'art," *Revue d'histoire littéraire de la France,* 1980, pp. 1027–39.

10. *L'Écho de Paris,* July 19, 1909 (NAF 15076, f. 132).

11. Montesquiou, "Le Séducteur," in *Altesses,* p. 78.

12. Lines from a poem Montesquiou sent to Boldini in June 1921, thanking him for the portrait of the poet he had executed in 1897 (fig. 95). This poem is preserved in the Museo Boldini, Ferrara (see *Giovanni Boldini,* exhib. cat., Paris, 1991, p. 116.)

13. Montesquiou, "L'Inextricable Graveur," in *Diptyque,* pp. 160, 195, 212.

14. Montesquiou, "Les Verres forgés," *Les Arts,* October 1910, pp. 31–32.

15. Montesquiou, "Fragments sur Constantin Guys," *Le Gaulois,* April 18, 1895.

16. Montesquiou, *Paul Helleu, peintre et graveur,* Paris, 1913, pp. 48–50.

17. *Idem,* pp. 45–46.

18. *Idem,* p. 48.

19. Montesquiou, "Monticelli," *Gazette des Beaux-Arts,* February 1901, pp. 91, 92, 104.

20. Montesquiou, *Exposition Gustave Moreau,* exhib. cat., Paris, 1906, p. 18.

21. *Idem,* pp. 29–30.

22. Transcribed from the manuscript in the Musée Gustave Moreau, Paris. The full text of the poem was published and analyzed by Joy Newton in "Robert de Montesquiou et Gustave Moreau," *Nottingham French Studies,* XV, No. 1, 1976, pp. 14–19.

23. Montesquiou, *Altesses,* p. 122.

24. Montesquiou, "Le Pavé rouge, Quelques Réflections sur 'l'Oeuvre' de M. Sargent," *Les Arts de la Vie,* June 3, 1905, pp. 333, 331–32.

25. Montesquiou, "Alfred Stevens," *Gazette des Beaux-Arts,* February 1900, pp. 104, 112-14.

26. Montesquiou, "Tissot Chrétien," *La Revue illustrée,* May 1896, pp. 324, 331.

The Garb

1. *La France,* May 17, 1894, NAF 15288, f. 126.

2. G. Geffroy, *La Justice,* June 1, 1894, NAF 15288, f. 128.

3. *Le Magasin littéraire de Gand,* July 19, 1894, NAF 15288, f. 129.

4. *Le Tintamarre,* May 20, 1894, NAF 15288, f. 127.

5. *Le Journal,* May 1, 1894, NAF 15288, f. 124.

6. *Gil Blas,* April 25, 1894, NAF 15288, f. 121.

7. C. Baudelaire, "Salon de 1846," in *Oeuvres complètes,* Paris, 1954, p. 678.

8. Baudelaire, *Oeuvres,* p. 907.

9. *The Times,* May 20, 1894, NAF 15288, f. 126.

10. J. Lorrain, "Chronique de Paris," *L'Évènement,* March 18, 1890, NAF 15038, f. 96.

11. "The Latest Duel," *Daily Graphic,* London, January 19, 1904, NAF 15063, f. 33.

12. Santillane [Jean Lorrain], "Lyres et épées," *Gil Blas,* June 10, 1897, NAF 15047, f. 52.

13. M. Cale, "La Vie qui passe, le carnet des heures," *L'Intransigeant,* July 1904, NAF 15063, f. 145.

14. Sem, "Vrai et faux chic, Ne Vous habillez pas richement," unidentified journal, 1909, NAF 15076, f. 109.

15. H. de Forge, "Le Poète méticuleux," *Le Courier du soir,* Verviers, December 20, 1921, NAF 15093, f. 264.

16. NAF 15097, f. 102.

17. NAF 15054, f. 116.

18. Cousteau, "Les Muses en Amérique," *La Vie parisienne,* January 1903, NAF 15053, f. 39.

19. M. Proust, *A la recherche du temps perdu,* Paris, 1954, II, p. 652.

20. F. Bac, *Intimités de la IIIè République, La Fin des "Temps délicieux," Souvenirs parisiens,* Paris, 1935, p. 171.

21. *La Petite Gironde,* December 19, 1921, NAF 15093, f. 262.

22. Information and photographs kindly provided by Lluis Reixach, Secretario General of the Fundación Gala-Salvador Dalí. Dalí's cane with the Montesquiou provenance had a handle richly set in *champlevé* enamels.

23. Duret, p. 100.

24. *La Vie parisienne,* May 29, 1894, NAF 15288, f. 127.

25. See M. Delbourg-Delphis, *Masculin singulier: Le Dandysme et son histoire,* Paris, 1985, p. 117.

26. L. Marsoleau, "En passant," *Le Rappel,* June 12, 1897, NAF 15047, f. 52.

27. M. Curtiss, *Other People's Letters: A Memoir,* Boston, 1978, p. 175. I am grateful to Claudia Pierpont for bringing this text to my attention.

28. Paris, private collection.

29. T. Veblen, *The Theory of the Leisure Class, An Economic Study of Institutions,* New York, 1919, pp. 170–71.

The Black Portraits

1. Newton 76.

2. Way, 1912, p. 115.

3. See Robertson, *Life,* p. 190.

4. Glasgow, LB 4/12, quoted in Young, MacDonald, and Spencer, text vol., p. 155, No. 315.

5. A. de Lostalot, "Salon de 1886," *Gazette des Beaux-Arts,* June 1886, p. 464.

6. "Current Art.—IV," *Magazine of Art,* VIII, 1885, pp. 467–68.

7. S. Starr, "Personal Recollections of Whistler," *Atlantic Monthly,* April 1908, p. 534.

8. R. de La Bretonne, *L'Écho de Paris,* May 16, 1895, NAF 15288, f. 131.

9. *Le Petit Parisien,* April 24, 1894, NAF 15288, f. 122.

10. P. Howard-Johnston, "Helleu et ses modèles," *La Nouvelle Revue des deux mondes,* December 1974, p. 609.

11. *Le Petit Parisien, loc. cit.*

12. *Le Magasin littéraire de Gand,* July 19, 1894, NAF 15288, f. 129.

13. *Le XIXè Siècle,* April 25, 1894, NAF 15288, f. 123.

14. *The Times,* May 20, 1894, NAF 15288, f. 126.

15. *Le Journal,* May 1, 1894, NAF 15288, f. 124.

16. *Le XIXè Siècle, loc. cit.*

17. *La France,* May 17, 1894, NAF 15288, f. 126.

18. *The New York Herald,* April 25, 1894, NAF 15288, f. 123.

19. Montesquiou, *Pas,* III, p. 256.

20. *Idem.* p. 229.

21. *Idem,* I, p. 211.

22. Jullian, p. 354.

23. Extracts from Alan Cole's diary in the Library of Congress, MSS Division, Pennell Whistler Collection, Box 281, PWC 281/679, PWC 281/686, PWC 281/662. I am grateful to Nigel Thorp for bringing the Cole diary to my attention and for transcribing the texts cited above.

24. G. Geffroy, "L'Exposition décanale de la peinture," *Vie artistique,* 1901, p. 129.

25. Glasgow, Whistler PH 3/9.

26. F. Villot, *Notice des tableaux exposés dans les galeries du Musée Impérial du Louvre,* Paris, 1855, No. 556; A. Brejon de Lavergnée and D. Thiébaut, *Catalogue sommaire illustré des peintures du Musée du Louvre,* Paris, 1981, II, p. 127, Inv. 942.

27. Glasgow, Whistler PH 3/5. Nigel Thorp kindly provided inventory references for the photographs of Velázquez' work that Whistler possessed.

28. Duret, p. 172.

29. Havemeyer, p. 213.

30. A. Personnaz, *Léon Bonnat,* Paris, 1923, p. 12.

31. A. Roquebert, in *1893, L'Europe des peintres,* exhib. cat., Paris, 1993, p. 244.

32. W. Rothenstein, *Men and Memories, Recollections,* New York, 1931, p. 121.

33. "Current Art," *Magazine of Art,* X, 1887, p. 111.

34. K. Cox, "Whistler and 'Absolute Painting,'" *Scribner's Magazine,* May 1904, pp. 637–38.

Index

Designed by Nathan Garland,
New Haven, Connecticut

Composed in a modern version
of Garamond by Ken Scaglia

Films by PFC,
Dole

Color separations by ART'NORD,
Aire-sur-la-Lys

Printed by CLERC S.A.,
Saint-Amand-Montrond

Bound by RELIURES BRUN,
Malesherbes

Printed and bound in France